Reflections from

POPE FRANCIS

JEREMY P. TARCHER/PENGUIN
a member of Penguin Group (USA)
New York

Reflections from
POPE FRANCIS

An Invitation to Journaling,
Prayer, and Action

✝

SUSAN STARK *and*
DANIEL J. PIERSON

Jeremy P. Tarcher/Penguin
Published by the Penguin Group
Penguin Group (USA) LLC
375 Hudson Street
New York, New York 10014

USA · Canada · UK · Ireland · Australia
New Zealand · India · South Africa · China

penguin.com
A Penguin Random House Company

Most Tarcher/Penguin books are available at special quantity discounts for bulk
purchase for sales promotions, premiums, fund-raising, and educational needs.
Special books or book excerpts also can be created to fit specific needs.
For details, write: Special.Markets@us.penguingroup.com.

ISBN 978-0-399-17320-2

Printed in the United States of America
1   3   5   7   9   10   8   6   4   2

BOOK DESIGN BY AMANDA DEWEY

To Maryana and the Madonna House community and to my family and friends: your prayers have helped guide this project. Many thanks.

—Susan Stark

For Dennis J. Geaney, O.S.A.,
Priest, Prophet, and Mentor

—Daniel J. Pierson

Reflections from

POPE FRANCIS

Introduction

To protect creation, to protect every man and every woman,
to look upon them with tenderness and love, is to open up a
horizon of hope; it is to let a shaft of light break through the
heavy clouds; it is to bring the warmth of hope!

POPE FRANCIS, HOMILY, SAINT PETER'S SQUARE,
TUESDAY, MARCH 19, 2013

Since Cardinal Jorge Mario Bergoglio's election as pope on March 13, 2013, the words and actions of Pope Francis have challenged and inspired people throughout the world. His simplicity, gentle spirit, openness, and humility are an inspiration not only to Catholics, but to people everywhere.

The world has embraced Pope Francis as a man of great faith and witness to the Gospel. He invites us to live lives of truth and simplicity, to seek goodness and beauty, and to act with justice and mercy. He challenges us to care for those who experience poverty, disaster, violence, and suffering, and to reach out with compassion to those who are most vulnerable, especially the young and the elderly. Pope Francis's reflections transcend all faith traditions. His words have universal appeal for all people seeking wisdom and hope on their spiritual journeys.

This book invites people into a spiritual reflection process that places the predominant themes of Pope Francis and of sacred scripture—such as mercy, peace, forgiveness, and hope—into conversation with their own life experiences and faith journeys. The reflections we have chosen can be used in a variety of ways: as daily or weekly reflections for one's own personal prayer, as prayers or meditations to begin a meeting or small group sharing, as a starting point to explore more deeply the source from which the reflection is taken, or as a focus for quiet time, spiritual reflection, and journaling.

The option of using the reflections as a basis for journaling through writing, sketching, or drawing can help people of all spiritual traditions discover the "heart of the matter," as it applies to their own lives. Here is a simple process:

1. Choose a reflection. You may want to start at the beginning—the reflections are organized chronologically from the beginning to the end of Pope Francis's first year as pope. Or, find a reflection whose theme resonates with something you are experiencing in your life right now—a thematic index appears at the back of the book. Or, randomly select a reflection.

2. Read the focusing statement that opens the reflection. Consider how it connects to your life, to your experience, to the world around you.

3. Read the reflection from Pope Francis. What is he saying? How do his words resonate with you? How do they challenge you, give you hope, encourage you to change or to take action in some aspect of your life?

4. Identify the heart of the matter—that which is most important and meaningful to you about what you have read. Let it inspire you to write, sketch, or draw.

5. Conclude your reflection time by prayerfully reading the Scripture passage.

Pope Francis has cast the net wide, speaking to the hearts of men, women, and children everywhere about the things in life that matter most. He reminds us that every person is worthy of our giving, every person reflects something of God's glory, every person is immensely holy and deserves our love (see Apostolic Exhortation, *Evangelii Gaudium*, Chapter 5, I, 274, November 24, 2013).

There is no doubt that Pope Francis is a great gift to the Catholic Church. But we also believe that he is a gift to all Christians and people of faith. So may all of our hearts be open, as Pope Francis implores, to the love and mercy of God. May our reflection be blessed and fruitful.

1. JOURNEY IN THE PRESENCE OF THE LORD

Our life is a journey, and when we stop moving, things go wrong. Always journeying, in the presence of the Lord, in the light of the Lord, seeking to live with the blamelessness that God asked of Abraham in His promise.

Homily, Sistine Chapel, Thursday, March 14, 2013
"Missa Pro Ecclesia" with the Cardinal Electors

✝

O house of Jacob, come, let us walk in the light of the LORD.

ISAIAH 2:5

2. PONDER THE PATIENCE GOD HAS FOR YOU

Ah! Brothers and Sisters, God's face is the face of a merciful father who is always patient. Have you thought about God's patience, the patience He has with each one of us? That is His mercy. He always has patience, patience with us, He understands us, He waits for us, He does not tire of forgiving us if we are able to return to Him with a contrite heart. "Great is God's mercy," says the Psalm.

Angelus, Saint Peter's Square, Sunday, March 17, 2013

The Lord is not slow about his promise, as some think of slowness, but is patient with you, not wanting any to perish, but all to come to repentance.

2 Peter 3:9

3. BE A PERSON OF MERCY

I think we too are people who, on the one hand want to listen to Jesus, but on the other hand, at times, like to find a stick to beat others with, to condemn others. And Jesus has this message for us: mercy. I think—and I say it with humility—that this is the Lord's most powerful message: mercy.

Homily, Parish of Saint Anna in the Vatican,
Fifth Sunday of Lent, March 17, 2013
Holy Mass

When the scribes of the Pharisees saw that he was eating with sinners and tax collectors, they said to his disciples, "Why does he eat with tax collectors and sinners?" When Jesus heard this, he said to them, "Those who are well have no need of a physician, but those who are sick; I have come to call not the righteous but sinners."

MARK 2:16–17

4. NEVER TIRE OF ASKING FOR FORGIVENESS

It is not easy to entrust oneself to God's mercy, because it is an abyss beyond our comprehension. But we must! "Oh, Father, if you knew my life, you would not say that to me!" "Why, what have you done?" "Oh, I am a great sinner!" "All the better! God to Jesus: He likes you to tell Him these things!" He forgets, He has a very special capacity for forgetting. He forgets, He kisses you, He embraces you and He simply says to you: "Neither do I condemn you; go, and sin no more" (John 8:11). That is the only advice He gives you . . . The Lord never tires of forgiving: never! It is we who tire of asking His forgiveness. Let us ask for the grace not to tire of asking forgiveness, because He never tires of forgiving. Let us ask for this grace.

Homily, Parish of Saint Anna in the Vatican, Fifth Sunday of Lent,
March 17, 2013
Holy Mass

And Jesus said, "Neither do I condemn you. Go your way, and from now on do not sin again."

JOHN 8:11

5. OPEN UP A HORIZON OF HOPE

Hoping against hope! Today too, amid so much darkness, we need to see the light of hope and to be men and women who bring hope to others. To protect creation, to protect every man and every woman, to look upon them with tenderness and love, is to open up a horizon of hope. It is to let a shaft of light break through the heavy clouds. It is to bring the warmth of hope.

Homily, Saint Peter's Square, Tuesday, March 19, 2013
Mass for the Beginning of the Petrine Ministry of the Bishop of Rome

†

May the God of hope fill you with all joy and peace in believing, so that
you may abound in hope by the power of the Holy Spirit.

ROMANS 15:13

6. BE PROTECTORS OF GOD'S GIFTS

The vocation of being a "protector," however, is not just something involving us Christians alone—it also has a prior dimension which is simply human, involving everyone. It means protecting all creation, the beauty of the created world, as the Book of Genesis tells us and as Saint Francis of Assisi showed us. It means respecting each of God's creatures and respecting the environment in which we live. It means protecting people, showing loving concern for each and every person, especially children, the elderly, those in need, who are often the last we think about. It means caring for one another in our families: husbands and wives first protect one another, and then, as parents, they care for their children, and children themselves, in time, protect their parents. It means building sincere friendships in which we protect one another in trust, respect, and goodness. In the end, everything has been entrusted to our protection, and all of us are responsible for it. Be protectors of God's gifts!

Homily, Saint Peter's Square, Tuesday, March 19, 2013
Mass for the Beginning of the Petrine Ministry of the Bishop of Rome

✝

God saw everything that he had made, and indeed, it was very good.

GENESIS 1:31

7. KEEP ALIVE THE
THIRST FOR GOD

The Church is likewise conscious of the responsibility which all of us have for our world, for the whole of creation, which we must love and protect. There is much that we can do to benefit the poor, the needy and those who suffer, and to favor justice, promote reconciliation and build peace. But before all else we need to keep alive in our world the thirst for the absolute, and to counter the dominance of a one-dimensional vision of the human person, a vision which reduces human beings to what they produce and to what they consume: this is one of the most insidious temptations of our time.

Address, Clementine Hall, Wednesday, March 20, 2013
Audience with Representatives of the Churches and Ecclesial Communities
and of the Different Religions

The LORD tests the righteous and the wicked,
and his soul hates the lover of violence.
On the wicked he will rain coals of fire and
sulfur;
a scorching wind shall be the portion of
their cup.
For the
LORD is righteous;
he loves righteous deeds;
the upright shall behold his face.

PSALM 11:5–7

8. LET JESUS CARRY YOU

Let us follow Jesus! We accompany, we follow Jesus, but above all we know that He accompanies us and carries us on His shoulders. This is our joy, this is the hope that we must bring to the world. Please do not let yourselves be robbed of hope! Do not let hope be stolen! The hope that Jesus gives us.

Homily, Saint Peter's Square, Sunday, March 24, 2013
Celebration of Palm Sunday of the Passion of Our Lord,
Twenty-Eighth World Youth Day

†

"Blessed is the king
who comes in the name of the Lord!
Peace in heaven,
and glory in the highest heaven!"

LUKE 19:38

9. SERVE OTHERS

A m I really willing, willing to serve, to help others?" Let us think about this, just this.

Homily, Prison for Minors "Casa del Marmo," Rome,
Holy Thursday, March 28, 2013
Mass of the Lord's Supper

†

"Truly I tell you, just as you did it to one of the least of these who are members of my family, you did it to me."

MATTHEW 25:40

10. NEVER GIVE UP

Dear brothers and sisters, let us not be closed to the newness that God wants to bring into our lives! Are we often weary, disheartened and sad? Do we feel weighed down by our sins? Do we think that we won't be able to cope? Let us not close our hearts, let us not lose confidence, let us never give up: there are no situations which God cannot change, there is no sin which He cannot forgive if only we open ourselves to Him.

Homily, Vatican Basilica, Holy Saturday, March 30, 2013
Easter Vigil

So if anyone is in Christ, there is a new creation: everything old has passed away; see, everything has become new!

2 CORINTHIANS 5:17

11. REMEMBER

To remember what God has done and continues to do for me, for us, to remember the road we have travelled—this is what opens our hearts to hope for the future. May we learn to remember everything that God has done in our lives.

Homily, Vatican Basilica, Holy Saturday, March 30, 2013
Easter Vigil

I will call to mind the deeds of the Lord; I will remember your wonders of old.

Psalm 77:11

12. LET GOD'S LOVE LIFT YOU UP AND LEAD YOU ON

What a beautiful truth of faith this is for our lives: the mercy of God! God's love for us is so great, so deep—it is an unfailing love, one which always takes us by the hand and supports us, lifts us up and leads us on.

Homily, Basilica of Saint John Lateran, Divine Mercy Sunday, April 7, 2013
Papal Mass for the Possession of the Chair of the Bishop of Rome

†

"His mercy is for those who fear him
from generation to generation."

LUKE 1:50

13. TRUST THAT GOD WAITS FOR YOU

God is patient with us because He loves us, and those who love are able to understand, to hope, to inspire confidence—they do not give up, they do not burn bridges, they are able to forgive. Let us remember this in our lives as Christians: God always waits for us, even when we have left Him behind! He is never far from us, and if we return to Him, He is ready to embrace us.

Homily, Basilica of Saint John Lateran, Divine Mercy Sunday, April 7, 2013
Papal Mass for the Possession of the Chair of the Bishop of Rome

†

"But while he was still far off, his father saw him and was filled with compassion; he ran and put his arms around him and kissed him . . ."

LUKE 15:20

14. ANSWER ADVERSITY WITH LOVE

When a person truly knows Jesus Christ and believes in Him, that person experiences His presence in life as well as the power of His Resurrection and cannot but communicate this experience. And if this person meets with misunderstanding or adversity, he behaves like Jesus in His Passion: he answers with love and with the power of the truth. . . . Brotherly love is the closest testimony we can give that Jesus is alive with us, that Jesus is risen.

Regina Cæli, Saint Peter's Square, Third Sunday of Easter, April 14, 2013

†

The high priest questioned them, saying, "We gave you strict orders not to teach in this name, yet here you have filled Jerusalem with your teaching and you are determined to bring this man's blood on us." But Peter and the apostles answered, "We must obey God rather than any human authority. The God of our ancestors raised up Jesus, whom you had killed by hanging him on a tree. God exalted him at his right hand as Leader and Savior that he might give repentance to Israel and forgiveness of sins. And we are witnesses to these things, and so is the Holy Spirit whom God has given to those who obey him."

ACTS 5:27–32

15. BE AN EVERYDAY SAINT

To be sure, the testimony of faith comes in very many forms, just as in a great fresco, there is a variety of colors and shades, yet they are all important, even those which do not stand out. In God's great plan, every detail is important, even yours, even my humble little witness, even the hidden witness of those who live their faith with simplicity in everyday family relationships, work relationships, friendships. There are the saints of everyday, the "hidden" saints, a sort of "middle class of holiness," as a French author said, that "middle class of holiness" to which we can all belong.

Homily, Basilica of Saint Paul Outside-the-Walls, Sunday, April 14, 2013
Eucharistic Celebration

Pursue peace with everyone, and the holiness without which no one will see the Lord. See to it that no one fails to obtain the grace of God; that no root of bitterness springs up and causes trouble, and through it many become defiled.

HEBREWS 12:14–15

16. PREACH WITH YOUR LIFE

Let us all remember this: one cannot proclaim the Gospel of Jesus without the tangible witness of one's life. Those who listen to us and observe us must be able to see in our actions what they hear from our lips, and so give glory to God! I am thinking now of some advice that Saint Francis of Assisi gave his brothers: preach the Gospel and, if necessary, use words. Preaching with your life, with your witness.

Homily, Basilica of Saint Paul Outside-the-Walls, Sunday, April 14, 2013
Eucharistic Celebration

—— ✝ ——

"'. . . for you will be his witness to all the world of what you have seen and heard.'"

ACTS 22:15

17. RECOGNIZE THE VOICE OF JESUS

Jesus wants to establish with His friends a relationship which mirrors His own relationship with the Father: a relationship of reciprocal belonging in full trust, in intimate communion. To express this profound understanding, this relationship of friendship, Jesus uses the image of the shepherd with his sheep: he calls them and they recognize his voice, they respond to his call and follow him. This parable is very beautiful! The mystery of his voice is evocative: only think that from our mother's womb we learn to recognize her voice and that of our father. It is from the tone of a voice that we perceive love or contempt, affection or coldness. Jesus's voice is unique! If we learn to distinguish it, He guides us on the path of life, a path that goes beyond even the abyss of death.

Regina Cæli, Saint Peter's Square, Fourth Sunday of Easter, April 21, 2013

✝

"The gatekeeper opens the gate for him, and the sheep hear his voice. He calls his own sheep by name and leads them out. When he has brought out all his own, he goes ahead of them, and the sheep follow him because they know his voice."

JOHN 10:3–4

18. LOVE SOMEONE
WELL TODAY

How marvelous it would be if, at the end of the day, each of us could say: today I have performed an act of charity towards others!

Via Twitter @Pontifex, Monday, April 29, 2013

Above all, clothe yourselves with love,
which binds everything together in perfect
harmony.

COLOSSIANS 3:14

19. SHOW A SIGN OF LOVE

How beautiful it would be if each of you, every evening, could say: Today at school, at home, at work, guided by God, I showed a sign of love towards one of my friends, my parents, an older person! How beautiful!

Homily, Saint Peter's Square, Sunday, April 28, 2013
Holy Mass and Conferral of the Sacrament of Confirmation

✝

Pursue love and strive for the spiritual gifts. . . .

1 CORINTHIANS 14:1

20. WALK WITH DETERMINATION

Do not be content to live a mediocre Christian life; walk with determination along the path of holiness.

Via Twitter @Pontifex, Tuesday, May 7, 2013

Pursue peace with everyone, and the holiness without which no one will
see the Lord.

HEBREWS 12:14

21. BE FAITHFUL

. . . how am I faithful to Christ? Let us take this question with us, to think about it during the day: how am I faithful to Christ? Am I able to make my faith seen with respect, but also with courage? Am I attentive to others, do I notice who is in need, do I see everyone as brothers and sisters to love?

Homily, Saint Peter's Square, Sunday, May 12, 2013
Holy Mass and Canonizations

✞

"Sanctify them in the truth; your word is truth. As you have sent me into the world, so I have sent them into the world."

JOHN 17:17–18

22. BE OPEN TO GOD'S SURPRISES

Newness always makes us a bit fearful, because we feel more secure if we have everything under control, if we are the ones who build, program, and plan our lives in accordance with our own ideas, our own comfort, our own preferences. This is also the case when it comes to God. Often we follow Him, we accept Him, but only up to a certain point. . . . Let us ask ourselves today: Are we open to "God's surprises"?

Homily, Saint Peter's Square, Sunday, May 19, 2013
Solemnity of Pentecost, Holy Mass with the Ecclesial Movements

But, as it is written,
"What no eye has seen, nor ear heard,
nor human heart conceived,
what God has prepared for those who love
    him. . . ."

1 CORINTHIANS 2:9

23. IMITATE GOD

God is good, let us imitate God.

Address, Clementine Hall, Friday, May 24, 2013
Participants in the Plenary of the Pontifical Council for the
Pastoral Care of Migrants and Itinerant People

Therefore be imitators of God, as beloved children, and live in love, as Christ loves us and gave himself up for us, a fragrant offering and sacrifice to God.

EPHESIANS 5:1-2

24. SEEK HUMILITY, SERVICE, AND LOVE

The world tells us to seek success, power, and money; God tells us to seek humility, service, and love.

Via Twitter @Pontifex, Sunday, June 2, 2013

"For all who exalt themselves will be humbled,
and those who humble themselves will be exalted."

LUKE 14:11

25. CARE FOR CREATION

Care of creation is not just something God spoke of at the dawn of history; He entrusts it to each of us as a part of His plan.

Via Twitter @Pontifex, Wednesday, June 5, 2013

✝

Ever since the creation of the world his eternal power and divine nature,
invisible though they are,
have been understood and seen through the things he has made.

ROMANS 1:20

26. SAY "YES" TO LOVE

Let us say "Yes" to love and not selfishness. Let us say "Yes" to life and not death. Let us say "Yes" to freedom and not enslavement to the many idols of our time. In a word, let us say "Yes" to God who is love, life, and freedom, and who never disappoints (cf. John 4:8; John 11:2; John 8:32). Let us say "Yes" to the God who is the Living One and the Merciful One.

Homily, Sunday, Saint Peter's Square, Sunday, June 16, 2013
Holy Mass for "Evangelium Vitae" Day

✝

"If you continue in my word, you are truly my disciples; and you will know the truth, and the truth will make you free."

JOHN 8:31–32

27. DECIDE TO BE A GOOD SAMARITAN

Human beings are not islands—we are a community. My thoughts turn to the well-known parable in the Gospel where a Samaritan helps someone in need. He is not prompted by philanthropy or the fact that he has money at his disposal, but by a desire to identify with the person he helps: he wants to share his lot. Indeed, after providing for the man's care, he announces that he will return to inquire after his health. What is involved here is more than mere compassion or perhaps a desire to share or to promote a reconciliation which can overcome differences and disagreements. It is a willingness to share everything and to decide to be Good Samaritans, instead of people who are indifferent before the needs of others.

Address, Clementine Hall, Thursday, June 20, 2013
38th Conference of the Food and Agriculture Organization of the United Nations (FAO)

"Which of these three, do you think, was a neighbor to the man who fell into the hands of the robbers?" He said, "The one who showed him mercy." Jesus said to him, "Go and do likewise."

Luke 10:36–37

28. SHARE YOUR GIFTS

Charity, patience, and tenderness are very beautiful gifts. If you have them, you want to share them with others.

Via Twitter @Pontifex, Wednesday, June 26, 2013

✝

. . . the fruit of the Spirit is love, joy, peace, patience, kindness, generosity, faithfulness, gentleness, and self-control.

GALATIANS 5:22-23

29. PRAY BRAVELY

If a person wants the Lord to grant a grace, he must go courageously and do what Abraham did with insistence, Jesus himself tells us we must pray like this . . . Abraham had been with the Lord for twenty-five years, he had acquired familiarity with him so he dared to embark on this form of prayer. Insistence, courage. It is tiring, but this is prayer. This is what receiving a grace from God is . . . Jesus teaches us: the Father knows things. Do not worry, the Father sends rain on the righteous and on sinners, He causes the sun to rise on the righteous and on sinners. I would like us all to take up the Bible, starting today, and to recite slowly Psalm 103 [102]: "Bless the Lord, O my soul" . . . Pray it all and in this way we will learn what to say to the Lord when we ask for a grace.

Morning Meditation, Chapel of the Domus Sanctae Marthae, Monday, July 1, 2013

Bless the Lord, O my soul,
and all this is within me,
bless his holy name.
Bless the Lord, O my soul, and do not forget
    all his benefits—
who forgives all your iniquity,
who heals all your diseases,
who redeems your life from the Pit,
who crowns you with steadfast love and
mercy,
who satisfies you with good as long as you
    live
so that your youth is renewed like the
    eagle's.

Psalm 103:1–5

30. BE A FULL-TIME CHRISTIAN

Christian life is not a collage of things. It is a harmonious totality, the work of the Holy Spirit. We cannot be Christian in bits and pieces, part-time Christians. We must be wholly Christian and full time.

Morning Meditation, Chapel of Domus Sanctae Marthae,
Saturday, July 6, 2013

✝

Little children, let us love, not in word or speech, but in truth and action . . . And this is his commandment, that we should believe in the name of his Son Jesus Christ and love one another, just as he has commanded us. All who obey his commandments abide in him, and he abides in them. And by this we know that he abides in us, by the Spirit that he has given us.

1 JOHN 3:18, 23–24

31. EXPERIENCE THE CONSOLATION OF GOD

Every Christian, and especially you and I, is called to be a bearer of this message of hope that gives serenity and joy: God's consolation, His tenderness towards all. But if we first experience the joy of being consoled by Him, of being loved by Him, then we can bring that joy to others. This is important if our mission is to be fruitful: to feel God's consolation and to pass it on to others!

Homily, Vatican Basilica, Sunday, July 7, 2013
Holy Mass with Seminarians, Novices, and Those Discerning Their Vocation

✝

Comfort, O comfort my people, says your God.

ISAIAH 40:1

32. TAKE RESPONSIBILITY

God is asking each of us: "Where is the blood of your brother which cries out to me?" Today no one in our world feels responsible—we have lost a sense of responsibility for our brothers and sisters. We have fallen into the hypocrisy of the priest and the levite whom Jesus described in the parable of the Good Samaritan: we see our brother half dead on the side of the road, and perhaps we say to ourselves: "poor soul . . . !" and then go on our way. It's not our responsibility, and with that we feel reassured, assuaged. The culture of comfort, which makes us think only of ourselves, makes us insensitive to the cries of other people, makes us live in soap bubbles which, however lovely, are insubstantial—they offer a fleeting and empty illusion which results in indifference to others. Indeed, it even leads to the globalization of indifference. In this globalized world, we have fallen into globalized indifference. We have become used to the suffering of others: it doesn't affect me, it doesn't concern me, it's none of my business!

We are a society which has forgotten how to weep, how to experience compassion—"suffering with" others: the globalization of indifference has taken from us the ability to weep! . . . "Has any one wept?" Today has anyone wept in our world?

Homily, "Arena" sports camp, Salina Quarter, Monday, July 8, 2013
Visit to Lampedusa

"Lord, when was it that we saw you hungry or thirsty or a stranger or naked or sick or in prison, and did not take care of you?" Then he will answer them, "Truly I tell you, just as you did not do it to one of the least of these, you did not do it to me."

Matthew 25:44–45

33. RISE TO THE PROMISE FOUND IN YOUNG PEOPLE

Listen! Young people are the window through which the future enters the world. They are the window, and so they present us with great challenges. Our generation will show that it can rise to the promise found in each young person when we know how to give them space. This means that we have to create the material and spiritual conditions for their full development. To give them a solid basis on which to build their lives. To guarantee their safety and their education to be everything they can be. To pass on to them lasting values that make life worth living. To give them a transcendent horizon for their thirst for authentic happiness and their creativity for the good. To give them the legacy of a world worthy of human life, and to awaken in them their greatest potential as builders of their own destiny, sharing responsibility for the future of everyone. If we can do all this, we anticipate today the future that enters the world through the window of the young.

Address, Garden of Guanabara Palace, Rio de Janeiro, Monday, July 22, 2013
Welcome Ceremony, Apostolic Journey to Rio de Janeiro
on the Occasion of the Twenty-Eighth World Youth Day

†

These are the things you must insist on and teach. Let no one despise your youth, but set the believers an example in speech and conduct, in love, in faith, in purity.

1 TIMOTHY 4:12

34. HONOR THE STRENGTH OF THE YOUNG AND THE WISDOM OF THE ELDERLY

A people have a future if it goes forward with both elements: with the young, who have the strength, and things move forward because they do the carrying, and with the elderly because they are the ones who give life's wisdom. And I have often thought that we do the elderly an injustice, we set them aside as if they had nothing to offer us. They have wisdom, life's wisdom, history's wisdom, the homeland's wisdom, the family's wisdom. And we need all this!

Papal Flight to Brazil, Monday, July 22, 2013
Apostolic Journey to Rio de Janeiro on the Occasion of the Twenty-Eighth
World Youth Day Meeting with the Journalists during the Flight to Brazil

Happy are those who find wisdom,
and those who get understanding,
for her income is better than silver,
and her revenue better than gold.
She is more precious than jewels,
and nothing you desire can compare
with her.

35. BE SURPRISED BY GOD'S LOVE

Anyone who is a man or a woman of hope—the great hope which faith gives us—knows that even in the midst of difficulties God acts and He surprises us . . . God always saves the best for us, but He asks us to let ourselves be surprised by His love, to accept His surprises. Let us trust God!

Homily, Basilica of the Shrine of Our Lady of the Conception of Aparecida,
Wednesday, July 24, 2013
Holy Mass, Apostolic Journey to Rio de Janeiro on the Occasion of the
Twenty-Eighth World Youth Day

†

"As the Father has loved me, so I have loved you; abide in my love."

JOHN 15:9

36. SPREAD JOY

Christians are joyful, they are never gloomy. God is at our side. . . . Jesus has shown us that the face of God is that of a loving Father. Sin and death have been defeated. Christians cannot be pessimists! They do not look like someone in constant mourning. If we are truly in love with Christ and if we sense how much He loves us, our hearts will "light up" with a joy that spreads to everyone around us.

Homily, Basilica of the Shrine of Our Lady of the
Conception of Aparecida, Wednesday, July 24, 2013
Holy Mass, Apostolic Journey to Rio de Janeiro on the
Occasion of the Twenty-Eighth World Youth Day

✝

The Lord has done great things for us,
and we rejoiced.

PSALM 126:3

37. BE LIGHTS OF HOPE!

How many difficulties are present in the life of every individual, among our people, in our communities? Yet as great as these may seem, God never allows us to be overwhelmed by them. In the face of those moments of discouragement we experience in life, in our efforts to evangelize or to embody our faith as parents within the family, I would like to say forcefully: Always know in your heart that God is by your side—He never abandons you! Let us never lose hope! Let us never allow it to die in our hearts! The "dragon," evil, is present in our history, but it does not have the upper hand. The one with the upper hand is God, and God is our hope! . . . Dear brothers and sisters, let us be lights of hope! Let us maintain a positive outlook on reality.

Homily, Basilica of the Shrine of Our Lady of the Conception of Aparecida,
Wednesday, July 24, 2013
Holy Mass, Apostolic Journey to Rio de Janeiro on the Occasion
of the Twenty-Eighth World Youth Day

Rejoice in hope, be patient in suffering, persevere in prayer.

ROMANS 12:12

38. PUT ON FAITH, HOPE, AND LOVE

. . . if we want [life] to have real meaning and fulfilment, as you want and as you deserve, I say to each one of you, "Put on faith," and life will take on a new flavor, life will have a compass to show you the way. "Put on hope" and every one of your days will be enlightened and your horizon will no longer be dark, but luminous. "Put on love," and your life will be like a house built on rock, your journey will be joyful, because you will find many friends to journey with you. Put on faith, put on hope, put on love! All together: "Put on faith," "Put on hope," "Put on love."

Greeting, Waterfront of Copacabana, Rio de Janeiro, Thursday, July 25, 2013
Welcoming Ceremony for the Young People,
Apostolic Journey to Rio de Janeiro on the Occasion of the
Twenty-Eighth World Youth Day

And now faith, hope, and love abide, these three; and the greatest of these is love.

1 Corinthians 13:13

39. HAVE AN ACTION PLAN

Please do not water down your faith in Jesus Christ. We dilute fruit drinks—orange, apple, or banana juice, but please do not drink a diluted form of faith. Faith is whole and entire, not something that you water down. It is faith in Jesus. It is faith in the Son of God made man, who loved me and who died for me. So then: make yourselves heard. Take care of the two ends of the population: the elderly and the young. Do not allow yourselves to be excluded and do not allow the elderly to be excluded. Secondly: do not "water down" your faith in Jesus Christ. The Beatitudes: What must we do, Father? Look, read the Beatitudes: that will do you good [see Matthew 5]. If you want to know what you actually have to do, read Matthew Chapter 25, which is the standard by which we will be judged. With these two things you have the action plan: the Beatitudes and Matthew 25. You do not need to read anything else. I ask you this with all my heart.

Address, Thursday, July 25, 2013
Meeting with Young People from Argentina, Apostolic Journey to Rio de Janeiro
on the Occasion of the Twenty-Eighth World Youth Day

✝

"Then the king will say to those at his right hand, 'Come, you that are blessed by my Father, inherit the kingdom prepared for you from the foundation of the world; for I was hungry and you gave me food, I was thirsty and you gave me something to drink, I was a stranger and you welcomed me, I was naked and you gave me clothing, I was sick and you took care of me, I was in prison and you visited me.'"

MATTHEW 25:34–36

40. GO AND BRING CHRIST

Where does Jesus send us? There are no borders, no limits: He sends us to everyone. The Gospel is for everyone, not just for some. It is not only for those who seem closer to us, more receptive, more welcoming. It is for everyone. Do not be afraid to go and to bring Christ into every area of your life, to the fringes of society, even to those who seem farthest away, most indifferent. The Lord seeks all, He wants everyone to feel the warmth of His mercy and love.

Homily, Waterfront of Copacabana, Rio de Janeiro, Sunday, July 28, 2013
Holy Mass, Apostolic Journey to Rio de Janeiro on the Occasion of the
Twenty-Eighth World Youth Day

"The harvest is plentiful, but the laborers are few; therefore ask the LORD of the harvest to send out laborers into his harvest."

MATTHEW 9:37-38

41. BUILD A NEW WORLD

Bringing the Gospel is bringing God's power to pluck up and break down evil and violence, to destroy and overthrow the barriers of selfishness, intolerance, and hatred, so as to build a new world. Dear young friends, Jesus Christ is counting on you! The Church is counting on you! The Pope is counting on you!

Homily, Waterfront of Copacabana, Rio de Janeiro, Sunday, July 28, 2013
Holy Mass, Apostolic Journey to Rio de Janeiro on the
Occasion of the Twenty-Eighth World Youth Day

The wolf shall live with the lamb,
the leopard shall lie down with the kid,
the calf and the lion and the fatling together,
and a little child shall lead them.
The cow and the bear shall graze,
their young shall lie down together;
and the lion shall eat straw like the ox.
The nursing child shall play over the hole of
the asp,
and the weaned child shall put its hand
on the adder's den.

ISAIAH 11:6–8

42. ENCOUNTER JESUS

I would like to ask you two questions. First: do you all have a desiring heart? A heart that desires? Think about it and respond silently in your hearts. I ask you is your heart filled with desire, or is it a closed heart, a sleeping heart, a heart numb to the things of life? The desire to go forward to encounter Jesus. The second question: where is your treasure, what are you longing for? Jesus told us: where your treasure is, there will be your heart—and I ask you: where is your treasure? What is the most important reality for you, the most precious reality, the one that attracts your heart like a magnet? What attracts your heart? May I say that it is God's love? Do you wish to do good to others, to live for the Lord and for your brothers and sisters? May I say this? Each one answer in his own heart.

Angelus, Saint Peter's Square, Sunday, August 11, 2013

✝

"For where your treasure is, there will your heart be also."

LUKE 12:34

43. GO FORWARD, WITH LOVE

This is the true treasure of humankind: going forward in life with love, with that love which the Lord has sown in our hearts, with God's love. This is the true treasure. But what is God's love? It is not something vague, some generic feeling. God's love has a name and a face: Jesus Christ, Jesus. Love for God is made manifest in Jesus. For we cannot love air. . . . Do we love air? Do we love all things? No, no we cannot, we love people and the person we love is Jesus, the gift of the Father among us. It is a love that gives value and beauty to everything else— a love that gives strength to the family, to work, to study, to friendship, to art, to all human activity. It even gives meaning to negative experiences, because this love allows us to move beyond these experiences, to go beyond them, not to remain prisoners of evil, it moves us beyond, always opening us to hope, that's it! Love of God in Jesus always opens us to hope, to that horizon of hope, to the final horizon of our pilgrimage. In this way our labors and failures find meaning. Even our sin finds meaning in the love of God because this love of God in Jesus Christ always forgives us. He loves us so much that He always forgives us.

Angelus, Saint Peter's Square, Sunday, August 11, 2013

✝

For God so loved the world that he gave his only Son, so that everyone who believes in him may not perish but may have eternal life.

JOHN 3:16

44. BELIEVE IN THE VICTORY OF LOVE

Hope is the virtue of those who, experiencing conflict—the struggle between life and death, good and evil—believe in the resurrection of Christ, in the victory of love.

We heard the Song of Mary, the *Magnificat*: it is the song of hope, it is the song of the People of God walking through history. It is the song many saints, men and women, some famous, and very many others unknown to us but known to God: mums, dads, catechists, missionaries, priests, sisters, young people, even children and grandparents: these have faced the struggle of life while carrying in their heart the hope of the little and the humble. Mary says: "My soul glorifies the Lord"—today, the Church too sings this in every part of the world. This song is particularly strong in places where the Body of Christ is suffering the Passion. For us Christians, wherever the Cross is, there is hope, always. If there is no hope, we are not Christian. That is why I like to say: do not allow yourselves to be robbed of hope. May we not be robbed of hope, because this strength is a grace, a gift from God which carries us forward with our eyes fixed on heaven.

Homily, Castel Gandolfo, Thursday, August 15, 2013
Holy Mass on the Solemnity of the Assumption of the Blessed Virgin Mary

"My soul magnifies the Lord,
And my spirit rejoices in God my Savior. . . ."

LUKE 1:46

45. CHOOSE TO FOLLOW JESUS

Remember this: following Jesus is not neutral, following Jesus means being involved, because faith is not a superficial decoration, it is a strength of the soul!

Angelus, Saint Peter's Square, Sunday, August 18, 2013

✝

"No one has greater love than this, to lay down one's life for one's friends. You are my friends if you do what I command you. . . . You did not choose me but I chose you. And I appointed you to go and bear fruit, fruit that will last, so that the Father will give you whatever you ask him in my name. I am giving you these commands so that you may love one another. If the world hates you, be aware that it hated me before it hated you. If you belonged to the world, the world would love you as its own. Because you do not belong to the world, but I have chosen you out of the world—therefore the world hates you."

JOHN 15:13–14, 16–19

46. CHOOSE GOODNESS, TRUTH, AND JUSTICE

Following Jesus entails giving up evil and selfishness and choosing good, truth and justice, even when this demands sacrifice and the renunciation of our own interests. And this indeed divides—as we know, it even cuts the closest ties. However, be careful: it is not Jesus who creates division! He establishes the criterion: whether to live for ourselves or to live for God and for others. To be served or to serve. To obey one's own ego or to obey God. It is in this sense that Jesus is a "sign that is spoken against" (Luke 2:34).

Angelus, Saint Peter's Square, Sunday, August 18, 2013

"Blessed are you when people revile you and persecute you and utter all kinds of evil against you falsely on my account. Rejoice and be glad, for your reward is great in heaven, for in the same way they persecuted the prophets who were before you."

MATTHEW 5:11–12

47. CHOOSE GOD AS THE CRITERION FOR YOUR LIFE

Faith means choosing God as the criterion and basis of life, and God is not empty, God is not neutral, God is always positive, God is love, and love is positive! After Jesus has come into the world it is impossible to act as if we do not know God, or as if He were something that is abstract, empty, a purely nominal reference. No, God has a real face, He has a name: God is mercy, God is faithfulness, He is life which is given to us all.

Angelus, Saint Peter's Square, Sunday, August 18, 2013

✝

"I came that they may have life, and have it abundantly."

JOHN 10:10

48. START THE BEAUTIFUL ADVENTURE OF DIALOGUE

. . . becoming acquainted with other people and other cultures is always good for us, it makes us grow. And why does this happen? It is because if we isolate ourselves we have only what we have, we cannot develop culturally. But, if we seek out other people, other cultures, other ways of thinking, other religions, we go out of ourselves and start that most beautiful adventure which is called "dialogue." Dialogue is very important for our own maturity, because in confronting another person, confronting other cultures, and also confronting other religions in the right way, we grow—we develop and mature. . . . This dialogue is what creates peace. It is impossible for peace to exist without dialogue.

Address, St. Damascus Courtyard in the Vatican, Wednesday, August 21, 2013
Students and Teachers from the Seibu Gakuen Bunri Junior High School
of Saitama, Tokyo (Japan)

Then Peter began to speak to them: "I truly understand that God shows no partiality, but in every nation anyone who fears him and does what is right is acceptable to him. You know the message he sent to the people of Israel, preaching peace by Jesus Christ—he is LORD of all."

ACTS 10:34–36

49. ENTER THROUGH JESUS'S DOOR

In our day we pass in front of so many doors that invite us to come in, promising a happiness which later we realize lasts only an instant, exhausts itself with no future. But I ask you: by which door do we want to enter? And who do we want to let in through the door of our life? I would like to say forcefully: let's not be afraid to cross the threshold of faith in Jesus, to let Him enter our life more and more, to step out of our selfishness, our closure, our indifference to others so that Jesus may illuminate our life with a light that never goes out. It is not a firework, not a flash of light! No, it is a peaceful light that lasts forever and gives us peace. Consequently it is the light we encounter if we enter through Jesus's door.

Angelus, Saint Peter's Square, Sunday, August 25, 2013

✝

"Ask, and it will be given you; search, and you will find; knock, and the door will be opened for you. For everyone who asks receives, and everyone who searches finds, and for everyone who knocks, the door will be opened."

MATTHEW 7:7–8

50. BE CHRISTIAN
BY THE TRUTH

I ask you: are you Christians by label or by the truth? And let each one answer within him—or herself! Not Christians, never Christians by label! Christians in truth, Christians in the heart. Being Christian is living and witnessing to faith in prayer, in works of charity, in promoting justice, in doing good. The whole of our life must pass through the narrow door which is Christ.

Angelus, Saint Peter's Square, Sunday, August 25, 2013

"Enter through the narrow gate; for the gate is wide and the road is easy that leads to destruction, and there are many who take it. For the gate is narrow and the road is hard that leads to life, and there are few who find it."

MATTHEW 7:13–14

51. SEEK THE GOOD OF OTHERS, CEASELESSLY

This, then, is the restlessness of love: ceaselessly seeking the good of the other, of the beloved, without ever stopping and with the intensity that leads even to tears. Then I think of Jesus weeping at the tomb of His friend Lazarus, of Peter who, after denying Jesus, encounters His gaze full of mercy and love, weeps bitterly, and of the father who waits on the terrace for his son's return and when he spies him still far off runs to meet him, the Virgin Mary comes to mind lovingly following her Son Jesus even to the Cross. Do we feel the restlessness of love? Do we believe in love for God and for others?

Homily, Basilica of Saint Augustine in Campo Marzio, Rome, Wednesday, August 28, 2013
Holy Mass for the Beginning of the General Chapter of the Order of Saint Augustine

Love is patient; love is kind; love is not envious or boastful or arrogant or rude. It does not insist on its own way; it is not irritable or resentful; it does not rejoice in wrongdoing, but rejoices in the truth. It bears all things, believes all things, hopes all things, endures all things.

1 CORINTHIANS 13:4–7

52. MAKE A WORLD
OF GOODNESS, BEAUTY,
AND TRUTH

Think about this carefully: putting your stakes on the great ideals, the ideal of making a world of goodness, beauty and truth. You can do this, you have the power to do it. If you do not do it, it is because of laziness.

Address, Vatican Basilica, Altar of the Chair, Wednesday, August 28, 2013
To the Young People from the Italian Diocese of Piacenza-Bobbio

✝

Surely goodness and mercy shall
follow me all the days of my life,
and I shall dwell in the house of the LORD
my whole life long.

PSALM 23:6

53. ASK FOR THE WISDOM OF DISCERNMENT

We should ask the Lord insistently for the wisdom of discernment in order to recognize when it is Jesus who gives us light and when it is the devil himself, disguised as an angel of light. Many believe they live in light but they are in darkness and are unaware of it! If we are meek in our inner light, we are gentle people, we hear the voice of Jesus in our heart, and look fearlessly at the Cross in the light of Jesus . . . We must always make the distinction: where Jesus is there is always humility, meekness, love and the Cross.

Morning Meditation, Chapel of Domus Sanctae Marthae,
Tuesday, September 3, 2013

Trust in the LORD with all your heart,
and do not rely on your own insight.
In all your ways acknowledge him,
and he will make straight your paths.

PROVERBS 3:5–6

54. KEEP JESUS AT THE CENTER

We encounter many Christians without Christ. For example, those like the Pharisees, Christians who put their faith, their religiosity, their Christianity, in laws: I must do this, I must do that. They are Christians out of habit, they do not know why they do it. . . . Where is Jesus? . . . If your devotions lead you to Jesus, then they are good. But if they leave you where you are, then something is wrong.

Morning Meditation, Chapel of Domus Sanctae Marthae,
Saturday, September 7, 2013

One Sabbath while Jesus was going through the grainfields, his disciples plucked some heads of grain, rubbed them in their hands, and ate them. But some of the Pharisees said, "Why are you doing what is not lawful on the sabbath?" Jesus answered, "Have you not read what David did when he and his companions were hungry? He entered the house of God and took and ate the bread of the Presence, which it is not lawful for any but the priests to eat, and gave some to his companions." Then he said to them, "The Son of Man is lord of the sabbath."

LUKE 6:1–5

55. WALK THE PATH OF PEACE

I s it possible to walk the path of peace? Can we get out of this spiral of sorrow and death? Can we learn once again to walk and live in the ways of peace? . . . From every corner of the world tonight, I would like to hear us cry out: Yes, it is possible for everyone! Or even better, I would like for each one of us, from the least to the greatest, including those called to govern nations, to respond: Yes, we want it! . . . violence and war are never the way to peace!

Let everyone be moved to look into the depths of his or her conscience and listen to that word which says: Leave behind the self-interest that hardens your heart, overcome the indifference that makes your heart insensitive towards others, conquer your deadly reasoning, and open yourself to dialogue and reconciliation. Look upon your brother's sorrow—I think of the children: look upon these . . . look at the sorrow of your brother, stay your hand and do not add to it, rebuild the harmony that has been shattered—and all this achieved not by conflict but by encounter!

Vigil of Prayer for Peace, Saint Peter's Square, Saturday, September 7, 2013

"Blessed are the peacemakers, for they will be called children of God."

Matthew 5:9

56. CHOOSE THE GOOD OF ALL

And God saw that it was good" (Genesis 1:12, 18, 21, 25). . . . our world, in the heart and mind of God, is the "house of harmony and peace," . . . the space in which everyone is able to find their proper place and feel "at home," because it is "good." God's world is a world where everyone feels responsible for the other, for the good of the other. . . . each of us deep down should ask ourselves: Is this really the world that I desire? Is this really the world that we all carry in our hearts? Is the world that we want really a world of harmony and peace, in ourselves, in our relations with others, in families, in cities, *in* and *between* nations? And does not true freedom mean choosing ways in this world that lead to the good of all and are guided by love?

Vigil of Prayer for Peace, Saint Peter's Square, Saturday, September 7, 2013

And God saw that it was good.

GENESIS 1:25

57. CONTEMPLATE JESUS SUFFERING

Only by contemplating the suffering humanity of Jesus can we become meek, humble, and tender as He is. There is no other way . . . hide your life in God with Christ. How can we bear witness? Contemplate Jesus. How can we forgive? Contemplate Jesus suffering. How can we not hate our neighbor? Contemplate Jesus suffering. How can we avoid gossiping about our neighbor? Contemplate Jesus suffering. There is no other way.

Morning Meditation, Chapel of Domus Sanctae Marthae,
Thursday, September 12, 2013

As God's chosen ones, holy and beloved, clothe yourselves with compassion, kindness, humility, meekness, and patience. Bear with one another and, if anyone has a complaint against another, forgive each other; just as the Lord has forgiven you, so you also must forgive.

COLOSSIANS 3:12–14

58. BE MERCIFUL

Jesus calls us all to follow this path: "Be merciful, even as your Father is merciful" (Luke 6:36). I now ask of you one thing. In silence, let's all think . . . everyone think of a person with whom we are annoyed, with whom we are angry, someone we do not like. Let us think of that person and in silence, at this moment, let us pray for this person and let us become merciful with this person.

Angelus, Saint Peter's Square, Sunday, September 15, 2013

†

"Be merciful, just as your Father is merciful."

59. PRAY FOR LEADERS

Let us pray for leaders that they govern us well. That they bring our homeland, our nations, our world, forward, to achieve peace and the common good. This word of God helps us to better participate in the common life of a people: those who govern, with the service of humility and love, and the governed, with participation, and especially prayer.

Morning Meditation, Chapel of Domus Sanctae Marthae,
Monday, September 16, 2013

✝

God also spoke to Moses and said to him: "I am the LORD. I appeared to Abraham, Isaac, and Jacob as God Almighty, but by my name 'The LORD' I did not make myself known to them. I also established my covenant with them. . . . and I have remembered my covenant. Say therefore to the Israelites, 'I am the LORD. . . . I will take you as my people, and I will be your God.'"

EXODUS 6:2–3, 6, 7

60. BEWARE OF THE TRAP OF IDOLATRY

Jesus told us clearly and definitively, that we cannot serve two masters—you cannot serve both God and money. It just doesn't work. There is something about the attitude of love towards money that takes us away from God. . . . It is the power of money that makes you deviate from authentic faith. It cuts you off from the faith, and weakens you so that you lose it . . . no one can redeem himself, or pay to God the appropriate price. The redemption of a life would be too expensive. No one can save themselves with money. . . . May the Lord help us all to not fall into the trap of idolatry of money.

Morning Meditation, Chapel of Domus Sanctae Marthae,
Friday, September 20, 2013

But those who want to be rich fall into temptation and are trapped by many senseless and harmful desires that plunge people into ruin and destruction.

1 TIMOTHY 6:9

61. BE COURAGEOUS

True charity requires courage: let us overcome our fear of getting our hands dirty so as to help those in need.

Via Twitter @Pontifex, Saturday, September 21, 2013

✝

"I have said this to you, so that in me you may have peace. In the world you face persecution. But take courage; I have conquered the world!"

JOHN 16:33

62. KNOCK AT THE DOOR OF GOD'S HEART

Mary prays, she prays together with the community of the disciples, and she teaches us to have complete trust in God and in His mercy. This is the power of prayer! Let us never tire of knocking at God's door. Every day through Mary let us carry our entire life to God's heart! Knock at the door of God's heart!

Homily, Square in the Front of the Shrine of Our Lady of Bonaria, Cagliari,
Sunday, September 22, 2013
Pastoral Visit to Cagliari, Holy Mass at the Shrine of Our Lady of Bonaria

All these were constantly devoting themselves to prayer, together with
certain women, including Mary the mother of Jesus, as well as his
brothers.

Acts 1:14

63. GIVE YOURSELF TO ANOTHER WITH LOVE

Love is free. Charity, love is life choice, it is a way of being, a way of life, it is a path of humility and of solidarity. There is no other way for this love: to be humble and in solidarity with others. . . . This word *solidarity* runs the risk of being deleted from the dictionary because it is a word that bothers us, it bothers us. Why? Because it requires you to look at another and give yourself to another with love. It is better to delete it from the dictionary because it bothers us. And as for us no, let us say: this is the way, humility and solidarity. Why? . . . It was Jesus—He said it! And we want to take this path. Christ's humility is not moralism or a feeling. Christ's humility is real—it is the choice of being small, of staying with the lowliest and with the marginalized, staying among all of us sinners. Be careful, this is not an ideology! It is a way of being and a way of life that comes from love and from God's heart.

Address, Cathedral of Cagliari, Sunday, September 22, 2013
Meeting with the Poor and Prison Inmates

✝

"By this everyone will know that you are my disciples,
if you have love for one another."

JOHN 13:35

64. PUT YOUR HEART INTO WORKS OF MERCY

Jesus is the path and *a path is for walking and following*. . . . I would like to encourage you to continue on this path, to move forward together, striving to preserve among you, first and foremost, charity. This is very important. We cannot follow Jesus on the path of love unless we first love others, unless we force ourselves to work together, to understand each other and to forgive each other, recognizing our own limits and mistakes. We must do works of mercy and with mercy! Putting our heart in them. Works of charity with love, with tenderness and always with humility!

Address, Cathedral of Cagliari, Sunday, September 22, 2013
Meeting with the Poor and Prison Inmates

✝

Surely goodness and mercy shall follow me all the days of my life,
and I shall dwell in the house of the LORD my whole life long.

PSALM 23:6

65. SERVE HUMBLY

Do you know what? Sometimes we also find arrogance in serving the poor! I am sure that you all have seen this—arrogance in serving those who are in need of our service. Some put on a show, they say what they do with the poor. Some exploit the poor for their own personal interests or the interests of the group. I know this, it is human but it is not right! This is not Jesus's way. And I will tell you more: this is a sin! It is a grave sin because it is using the poor, those who are in need, who are Jesus's flesh, for my own vanity. I use Jesus for my vanity and this is a grave sin! It would be better if these people stayed at home!

Address, Cathedral of Cagliari, Sunday, September 22, 2013
Meeting with the Poor and Prison Inmates

I therefore, the prisoner in the Lord,
beg you to lead a life worthy of the calling
to which you have been called,
with all humility and gentleness, with
    patience,
bearing with one another in love,
making every effort
to maintain the unity of the Spirit
in the bond of peace.

EPHESIANS 4:1–3

66. HAVE HOPE

Pessimistic Christians: how awful! You young people can't and mustn't be lacking in hope, hope is part of your being. A young person without hope is not young but has aged prematurely! Hope is part of your youth! If you don't have any hope, think seriously, think seriously. . . . A young person without joy and without hope is upsetting: he is not young. And when a young person has no joy, when he lacks confidence in life or loses hope, where can he go to find a bit of tranquility, a bit of peace? Without trust, without hope and without joy? You know, the merchants of death, these merchants that sell death, offer you a way out when you are sad, when you are without hope, without trust and disheartened! Please don't sell your youth to these people who sell death! All of you know what I'm talking about! You have all got it: don't sell!

Address, Largo Carlo Felice, Cagliari, Sunday, September 22, 2013
Pastoral Visit to Cagliari, Meeting with the Young People

✝

Rejoice in hope, be patient in suffering, persevere in prayer.

ROMANS 12:12

67. PUT OUT INTO THE DEEP!

The Lord is always with us. He comes to the shores of the sea of our life, He makes himself close to our failures, our frailty, and our sins in order to transform them. Never stop staking yourselves on Him, over and over again, as good sportsmen—some of you know this well from experience—who can face the strain of training in order to achieve results! Difficulties must not frighten you but on the contrary spur you to go beyond them. Hear Jesus's words as though they were addressed to you: put out into the deep and let down your nets . . . Put out into the deep! . . . Following Jesus is demanding, it means not being satisfied with small goals of little account but aiming on high with courage!

Address, Largo Carlo Felice, Cagliari, Sunday, September 22, 2013
Pastoral Visit to Cagliari, Meeting with the Young People

✝

When he had finished speaking, he said to Simon,
"Put out into the deep water and let down your nets for a catch."

LUKE 5:4

68. TAKE A FEW STEPS OUTSIDE YOURSELF

Put out into the deep, go out of yourselves: go out of our small world and open ourselves to God, to open ourselves increasingly also to our brethren. Opening ourselves to God is opening ourselves to others. Take a few steps outside ourselves, little steps, but take them. Little steps, going out of yourselves toward God and toward others, opening your heart to brotherhood, to friendship, and to solidarity.

Address, Largo Carlo Felice, Cagliari, Sunday, September 22, 2013
Pastoral Visit to Cagliari, Meeting with the Young People

"Master, we have worked all night long but have caught nothing. Yet if you say so, I will let down the nets."

LUKE 5:5

69. GO FORWARD, WITH JESUS

Let's stay united in prayer. And journey on in this life with Jesus: the saints did it.

Saints are like this: they are not born perfect, already holy! They become so because, like Simon Peter they trust in the word of the Lord and "put out into the deep." . . . They are ordinary people who instead of complaining "let down their nets for a catch." Imitate their example, entrust yourselves to their intercession and always be men and women of hope! No complaining! No discouragement! Never be depressed, never go to purchase comfort from death: none of it! Go forward with Jesus! He never fails, He never disappoints, He is loyal!

Address, Largo Carlo Felice, Cagliari, Sunday, September 22, 2013
Pastoral Visit to Cagliari, Meeting with the Young People

†

When they had done this, they caught so many fish that their nets were beginning to break. So they signaled their partners in the other boat to come and help them. And they came and filled both boats, so that they began to sink. . . . Then Jesus said to Simon, "Do not be afraid; from now on you will be catching people." When they had brought their boats to shore, they left everything and followed him.

LUKE 5:6–7, 10–11

70. LET GOD WRITE YOUR HISTORY

God, who has no history since He is eternal, wanted to make history, to walk close to His people. But there is more: He wanted to make Himself one of us and as one of us walk with us in Jesus . . . Walking with God's people, walking with sinners, even walking with the proud: how much the Lord did in order to help the proud hearts of the Pharisees. He wanted to walk. Humility. God always waits, God is beside us. God walks with us. He is humble. He waits for us always. Jesus always waits for us. This is the humility of God. . . . And if God entered into our history, let us also enter a little into His history or at least ask of Him the grace to let Him write history. May He write our history. It is a reliable one.

Morning Meditation, Chapel of Domus Sanctae Marthae,
Tuesday, September 24, 2013

In the beginning was the Word, and the Word was with God, and the Word was God. He was in the beginning with God. All things came into being through him, and without him not one thing came into being. What has come into being in him was life, and the life was the light of all people. The light shines in the darkness, and the darkness did not overcome it.

JOHN 1:1–4

71. BE LEAVENING

We have to be a leavening of life and love and the leavening is infinitely smaller than the mass of fruits, flowers, and trees that are born out of it. I believe I have already said that our goal is not to proselytize but to listen to needs, desires, and disappointments—despair, hope. We must restore hope to young people, help the old, be open to the future, spread love. Be poor among the poor. We need to include the excluded and preach peace.

Interview with Eugenio Scalfari, Founder of La Repubblica, *at the Pope's Residence,*
Tuesday, September 24, 2013
As Reported in news.va (Official Vatican Network)

Do you not know that a little yeast leavens the whole batch of dough?

1 Corinthians 5:6

72. TALK TO JESUS

You cannot know Jesus without having problems . . . by sitting in first class . . . in the calm . . . in the library. We only come to know Jesus on the daily path of life. . . . in order to know Jesus, we need to enter into a dialogue with Him. By talking with Him, in prayer, on our knees. If you don't pray, if you don't talk to Jesus, you don't know Him. It is by following Him, by going with Him, by walking with Him, by travelling along the road of His ways.

Morning Meditation, Chapel of Domus Sanctae Marthae,
Thursday, September 26, 2013

Let the word of Christ dwell in you richly; teach and admonish one another in all wisdom; and with gratitude in your hearts sing psalms, hymns, and spiritual songs to God. And whatever you do, in word or deed, do everything in the name of the Lord Jesus, giving thanks to God the Father through him.

COLOSSIANS 3:16–17

73. ACCEPT YOUR CROSS

There is no fruitful apostolic work without the Cross. . . . What will happen to me? What will my cross be like? We do not know, but there will be a cross, and we need to ask for the grace not to flee when it comes. Of course it scares us, but this is precisely where following Jesus takes us. Jesus's words to Peter come to mind: "Do you love me? Feed . . . Do you love me? Tend . . . Do you love me? Feed . . ." (cf. John 21:15–19) And these were among His last words to him: "They will carry you where you do not wish to go." He was announcing the Cross.

Morning Meditation, Chapel of Domus Sanctae Marthae,
Saturday, September 28, 2013

We know that our old self was crucified with him so that the body of sin might be destroyed, and we might no longer be enslaved to sin. For whoever has died is freed from sin. But if we have died with Christ, we believe that we will also live with him. We know that Christ, being raised from the dead, will never die again; death no longer has dominion over him. The death he died, he died to sin, once for all; but the life he lives, he lives to God. So you also must consider yourselves dead to sin and alive to God in Christ Jesus.

ROMANS 6:6–11

74. AWAKEN THE MEMORY OF GOD IN YOUR LIFE

. . . faith contains our own memory of God's history with us, the memory of our encountering God who always takes the first step, who creates, saves and transforms us. Faith is remembrance of His word which warms our heart, and of His saving work which gives life, purifies us, cares for and nourishes us.

Homily, Saint Peter's Square, Sunday, September 29, 2013
Holy Mass on the Occasion of the "Day for Catechists" During the Year of Faith

✝

"... for he has looked with favor on the
lowliness of his servant.
Surely, from now on all generations will
call me blessed;
for the Mighty One has done great things
for me,
and holy is his name."

LUKE 1:48–49

75. HONOR YOUR PARENTS AND THE ELDERLY

. . . a people who do not take care of their elderly and their children have no future because they will not have memory and will not have a promise. . . . the only commandment which brings with it a blessing is the fourth, the commandment which regards honoring our parents and the elderly.

Morning Meditation, Chapel of Domus Sanctae Marthae,
Monday, September 30, 2013

✝

Honor your father and your mother, so that your days may be long in the land that the LORD your God is giving you.

EXODUS 20:12

76. SEEK GOD IN EVERY HUMAN LIFE

I have a dogmatic certainty: God is in every person's life. God is in everyone's life. Even if the life of a person has been a disaster, even if it is destroyed by vices, drugs, or anything else—God is in this person's life. You can, you must try to seek God in every human life. Although the life of a person is a land full of thorns and weeds, there is always a space in which the good seed can grow. You have to trust God.

From the Interview with Pope Francis by Antonio Spadaro, S.J.
America Press, September 30, 2013

So God created humankind in his image,
In the image of God he created them;
male and female he created them.
God blessed them . . .

GENESIS 1:27–28

77. WORSHIP GOD AND SERVE OTHERS

The Lord always goes ahead, making the way of a Christian known to us. It is not . . . a path of revenge. The Christian spirit is something else, the Lord says. It is the spirit that He showed us in the most important moment of His life, in His passion: a spirit of humility, a spirit of meekness. . . . it is good for us to think about this spirit of humility, tenderness, and goodness. We all desire to share in the Lord's spirit of meekness. Where is the strength that brings us to this spirit? It is truly in love, in charity, in the awareness that we are in the hands of the Father. . . . Charity is simple: worshiping God and serving others.

Morning Meditation, Chapel of Domus Sanctae Marthae, Tuesday, October 1, 2013

He said to them, "'You shall love the Lord your God with all your heart, and with all your soul, and with all your mind.' This is the greatest and first commandment. And a second is like it: 'You shall love your neighbor as yourself.'"

MATTHEW 22:37–39

78. RESPECT CREATION

Let us respect creation, let us not be instruments of destruction! Let us respect each human being. May there be an end to armed conflicts which cover the earth with blood, may the clash of arms be silenced, and everywhere may hatred yield to love, injury to pardon, and discord to unity. Let us listen to the cry of all those who are weeping, who are suffering and who are dying because of violence, terrorism, or war, in the Holy Land, so dear to Saint Francis, in Syria, throughout the Middle East and everywhere in the world.

We turn to you, Francis, and we ask you: Obtain for us God's gift of harmony, peace, and respect for creation!

Homily, Saint Francis Square, Assisi, Friday, October 4, 2013

The heavens are telling the glory of God;
and the firmament proclaims his handiwork.

PSALM 19:1

79. RESIST THE TEMPTATION TO RUN AWAY FROM GOD

We can run away from God, as a Christian, as a Catholic, even as a priest, bishop, or Pope. We can all flee from God. This is a daily temptation: not to listen to God, not to hear His voice, not to hear His promptings, His invitation in our hearts.

Morning Meditation, Chapel of Domus Sanctae Marthae,
Monday, October 7, 2013

O God, you are my God, I seek you,
my soul thirsts for you;
my flesh faints for you,
as in a dry and weary land where there is no
water.

PSALM 63:1

80. FIND THE WORD OF GOD IN THE HISTORY OF EACH DAY

. . . and I also ask you: do we allow God to write the history of our lives or do we want to write it? This speaks to us of docility: are we docile to the Word of God? Yes, I want to be docile, but are you able to listen to [His Word], to hear it? Are you able to find the Word of God in the history of each day, or do your ideas so govern you that you do not allow the Lord to surprise you and speak to you?

Morning Meditation, Chapel of Domus Sanctae Marthae,
Monday, October 7, 2013

Let the word of Christ dwell in you richly; teach and admonish one another in all wisdom; and with gratitude in your hearts sing psalms, hymns, and spiritual songs to God. And whatever you do, in word or deed, do everything in the name of the Lord Jesus, giving thanks to God the Father through him.

COLOSSIANS 3:16–17

81. BE SURPRISED BY GOD

Today let us all ask ourselves whether we are afraid of what God might ask, or of what He does ask. Do I let myself be surprised by God, as Mary was, or do I remain caught up in my own safety zone: in forms of material, intellectual, or ideological security, taking refuge in my own projects and plans? Do I truly let God into my life? How do I answer Him?

Homily, Saint Peter's Square, Sunday, October 13, 2013
Holy Mass for the Marian Day on the Occasion of the Year of Faith

"Greetings, favored one! The Lord is with you." But she was much perplexed by his words and pondered what sort of greeting this might be. The angel said to her, "Do not be afraid, Mary, for you have found favor with God. And now, you will conceive in your womb and bear a son, and you will name him Jesus." . . . Then Mary said, "Here am I, the servant of the Lord; let it be with me according to your word."

LUKE 1:28–31, 38

82. REACH FOR THE LORD'S OUTSTRETCHED HAND

And I ask myself: Am I a Christian by fits and starts, or am I a Christian full-time? Our culture of the ephemeral, the relative, also takes its toll on the way we live our faith. God asks us to be faithful to Him, daily, in our everyday life. He goes on to say that, even if we are sometimes unfaithful to Him, He remains faithful. In His mercy, He never tires of stretching out His hand to lift us up, to encourage us to continue our journey, to come back and tell Him of our weakness, so that He can grant us His strength. This is the real journey: to walk with the Lord always, even at moments of weakness, even in our sins. Never to prefer a makeshift path of our own. That kills us. Faith is ultimate fidelity, like that of Mary.

Homily, Saint Peter's Square, Sunday, October 13, 2013
Holy Mass for the Marian Day on the Occasion of the Year of Faith

✝

. . . if we endure, we will also reign with him . . .

2 TIMOTHY 2:12

83. SAY "THANK YOU"

Everything is His gift. If we can realize that everything is God's gift, how happy will our hearts be? Everything is His gift. He is our strength! Saying "thank you" is such an easy thing, and yet so hard! How often do we say "thank you" to one another in our families? These are essential words for our life in common. "Sorry," "excuse me," "thank you." If families can say these three things, they will be fine. "Sorry," "excuse me," "thank you." How often do we say "thank you" in our families? How often do we say "thank you" to those who help us, those close to us, those at our side throughout life? All too often we take everything for granted! This happens with God too. It is easy to approach the Lord to ask for something, but to go and thank Him: "Well, I don't need to."

Homily, Saint Peter's Square, Sunday, October 13, 2013
Holy Mass for the Marian Day on the Occasion of the Year of Faith

"My soul magnifies the Lord,
and my spirit rejoices in God my savior."

84. PRAY ALWAYS

God invites us to pray insistently not because He is unaware of our needs or because He is not listening to us. On the contrary, He is always listening and He knows everything about us lovingly. On our daily journey, especially in times of difficulty, in the battle against the evil that is outside and within us, the Lord is not far away, He is by our side. We battle with Him beside us, and our weapon is prayer, which makes us feel His presence beside us, His mercy and also His help. . . .

Pray always, but not in order to convince the Lord by dint of words! He knows our needs better than we do! Indeed persevering prayer is the expression of faith in a God who calls us to fight with Him every day and at every moment in order to conquer evil with good.

Angelus, Saint Peter's Square, Sunday, October 20, 2013

✝

Rejoice always, pray without ceasing, give thanks in all circumstances; for this is the will of God in Christ Jesus for you.

1 Thessalonians 5:16–18

85. CENTER YOUR LIFE
ON THE LORD

If money and material things become the center of our lives, they seize us and make us slaves.

Via Twitter @Pontifex, Tuesday, October 29, 2013

I am the LORD your God, who brought you out of the land of Egypt, out of the house of slavery, you shall have no other gods before me. You shall not make for yourself an idol.

DEUTERONOMY 5:6–8

86. WALK THE WAY OF HOLINESS

Never hate, but serve others, the most needy—pray and live in joy. This is the way of holiness! . . . Holiness is a vocation for everyone. Thus we are all called to walk on the path of holiness, and this path has a name and a face: the face of Jesus Christ. He teaches us to become saints. . . . In fact, the Kingdom of Heaven is for those who do not place their security in material things but in love for God, for those who have a simple, humble heart that does not presume to be just and does not judge others, for those who know how to suffer with those who suffer and how to rejoice when others rejoice. They are not violent but merciful and strive to be instruments for reconciliation and peace.

Angelus, Saint Peter's Square, Sunday, November 1, 2013
Solemnity of All Saints

"Blessed are the merciful, for they will receive mercy. . . . Blessed are the peacemakers, for they will be called children of God."

87. BE AMAZED BY GOD'S
LOVE AND MERCY

The life that God prepares for us is not a mere embellishment of the present one: it surpasses our imagination, for God continually amazes us with His love and with His mercy. . . . If we look at things from only a human perspective, we tend to say that man's journey moves from life to death. This is what we see! But this is only so if we look at things from a human perspective. Jesus turns this perspective upside down and states that our pilgrimage goes from death to life: the fullness of life! We are on a journey, on a pilgrimage toward the fullness of life, and that fullness of life is what illumines our journey! Therefore death stands behind us, not before us. Before us is the God of the living, the God of the covenant, the God who bears my name, our names stand before us, as He said: "I am the God of Abraham, of Isaac, of Jacob," and also the God with my name, with your name . . . with our names. The God of the living! . . . Before us stands the final defeat of sin and death, the beginning of a new time of joy and of endless light . . . faithfulness is eternal, it cannot change. God's love is eternal, it cannot change! It is not only for a time: it is forever! It is for going forward! He is faithful forever and He is waiting for us, each one of us, He accompanies each one of us with His eternal faithfulness.

Angelus, Saint Peter's Square, Sunday, November 10, 2013

"Now he is God not of the dead, but of the living; for to him all of them are alive."

LUKE 20:38

88. GO FORWARD ON THE PATH OF HOPE

B y your endurance you will gain your lives" (Luke 21:19). There is so much hope in these words! They are a call to hope and patience, to be able to wait for the certain fruits of salvation, trusting in the profound meaning of life and of history: the trials and difficulties are part of the bigger picture—the Lord, the Lord of history, leads all to fulfillment. Despite the turmoil and disasters that upset the world, God's design of goodness and mercy will be fulfilled! And this is our hope: go forward on this path, in God's plan which will be fulfilled. This is our hope.

Angelus, Saint Peter's Square, Sunday, November 17, 2013

✝

"By your endurance you will gain your souls."

LUKE 21:19

89. KEEP MEMORY ALIVE

. . . we must not forget that the young and the old each holds a great wealth: both are the future of a people.

The young are the strength to go forward—the elderly retain the memory and wisdom of a people. There can be no authentic development, nor harmonious growth of a society if the power of the young and the memory of the old is denied. A people that fails to care for the young and the old has no future. This is why we need to do everything possible to ensure that our society does not develop social dross, and we must all commit ourselves to keeping our memory alive, with our gaze turned to the future.

Video Message, Verona, Italy, November 21–24, 2013
Third Festival of the Social Doctrine of the Church

Wisdom is radiant and unfading,
and she is easily discerned by those who
love her,
and is found by those who seek her.
She hastens to make herself known to those
who desire her.

WISDOM OF SOLOMON 6:12

90. SPREAD GOODNESS

Goodness always tends to spread. Every authentic experience of truth and goodness seeks by its very nature to grow within us, and any person who has experienced a profound liberation becomes more sensitive to the needs of others. As it expands, goodness takes root and develops. If we wish to lead a dignified and fulfilling life, we have to reach out to others and seek their good.

Apostolic Exhortation, Evangelii Gaudium, *II, 9, November 24, 2013*
On the Proclamation of the Gospel in Today's World

✝

For the love of Christ urges us on . . .

2 Corinthians 5:14

91. ENCOUNTER THE LORD

I invite all Christians, everywhere, at this very moment, to a renewed personal encounter with Jesus Christ, or at least an openness to letting Him encounter them. I ask all of you to do this unfailingly each day. No one should think that this invitation is not meant for him or her, since "no one is excluded from the joy brought by the Lord." The Lord does not disappoint those who take this risk. Whenever we take a step towards Jesus, we come to realize that He is already there, waiting for us with open arms. Now is the time to say to Jesus: "Lord, I have let myself be deceived; in a thousand ways I have shunned your love, yet here I am once more, to renew my covenant with you. I need you. Save me once again, Lord, take me once more into your redeeming embrace." How good it feels to come back to Him whenever we are lost! Let me say this once more: God never tires of forgiving us. We are the ones who tire of seeking His mercy.

Apostolic Exhortation, Evangelii Gaudium, *I, 3, November 24, 2013*
On the Proclamation of the Gospel in Today's World

✝

Sing for joy, O heavens, and exult, O earth;
break forth, O mountains, into singing!
For the Lord has comforted his people,
and will have compassion on his
suffering ones.

ISAIAH 49:13

92. TAKE A STEP FORWARD
IN LOVE

Let us ask the Lord to help us understand the law of love. How good it is to have this law! How much good it does us to love one another, in spite of everything. Yes, in spite of everything! Saint Paul's exhortation is directed to each of us: "Do not be overcome by evil, but overcome evil with good" (Romans 12:21). And again: "Let us not grow weary in doing what is right" (Galatians 6:9). We all have our likes and dislikes, and perhaps at this very moment we are angry with someone. At least let us say to the Lord: "Lord, I am angry with this person, with that person. I pray to you for him and for her." To pray for a person with whom I am irritated is a beautiful step forward in love, and an act of evangelization. Let us do it today! Let us not allow ourselves to be robbed of the ideal of fraternal love!

Apostolic Exhortation, Evangelii Gaudium, *Chapter Two, II, 101, November 24, 2013*
On the Proclamation of the Gospel in Today's World

So let us not grow weary in doing what is right . . .
whenever we have an opportunity,
let us work for the good of all . . .

GALATIANS 6:9, 10

93. BRING THE LOVE OF JESUS TO OTHERS

Being a disciple means being constantly ready to bring the love of Jesus to others, and this can happen unexpectedly and in any place: on the street, in a city square, during work, on a journey.

Apostolic Exhortation, Evangelii Gaudium, *Chapter Three, III, 127, November 24, 2013*
On the Proclamation of the Gospel in Today's World

†

"This is my commandment,
that you love one another as I have loved you."

John 15:12

94. OPEN YOUR HEART

When we live out a spirituality of drawing nearer to others and seeking their welfare, our hearts are opened wide to the Lord's greatest and most beautiful gifts. Whenever we encounter another person in love, we learn something new about God. Whenever our eyes are opened to acknowledge the other, we grow in the light of faith and knowledge of God. . . . This openness of the heart is a source of joy, since "it is more blessed to give than to receive" (Acts 20:35). We do not live better when we flee, hide, refuse to share, stop giving and lock ourselves up in our own comforts. Such a life is nothing less than slow suicide.

Apostolic Exhortation, Evangelii Gaudium, *Chapter Five, I, 272, November 24, 2013*
On the Proclamation of the Gospel in Today's World

In all this I have given you an example that by such work we must support the weak, remembering the words of the Lord Jesus, for he himself said,
"It is more blessed to give than to receive."

ACTS 20:35

95. HELP ONE PERSON
HAVE A BETTER LIFE

If we are to share our lives with others and generously give of ourselves, we also have to realize that every person is worthy of our giving. Not for their physical appearance, their abilities, their language, their way of thinking, or for any satisfaction that we might receive, but rather because they are God's handiwork, His creation. God created that person in His image, and he or she reflects something of God's glory. Every human being is the object of God's infinite tenderness, and He Himself is present in their lives. Jesus offered His precious blood on the cross for that person. Appearances notwithstanding, every person is immensely holy and deserves our love. Consequently, if I can help at least one person to have a better life, that already justifies the offering of my life. It is a wonderful thing to be God's faithful people. We achieve fulfilment when we break down walls and our heart is filled with faces and names!

Apostolic Exhortation, Evangelii Gaudium, *Chapter Five, I, 274, November 24, 2013*
On the Proclamation of the Gospel in Today's World

For it was you who formed my inward parts;
you knit me together in my mother's womb.
I praise you, for I am fearfully and
wonderfully made.
Wonderful are your works;
that I know very well.

Psalm 139:13–14

96. BELIEVE THAT THE KINGDOM OF GOD IS ALREADY PRESENT

Let us believe the Gospel when it tells us that the Kingdom of God is already present in this world and is growing, here and there, and in different ways: like the small seed which grows into a great tree (cf. Matthew 13:31–32), like the measure of leaven that makes the dough rise (cf. Matthew 13:33) and like the good seed that grows amid the weeds (cf. Matthew 13:24–30) and can always pleasantly surprise us. The Kingdom is here, it returns, it struggles to flourish anew. Christ's resurrection everywhere calls forth seeds of that new world—even if they are cut back, they grow again, for the resurrection is already secretly woven into the fabric of this history, for Jesus did not rise in vain. May we never remain on the sidelines of this march of living hope!

Apostolic Exhortation, Evangelii Gaudium, *Chapter Five, I, 278, November 24, 2013*
On the Proclamation of the Gospel in Today's World

"The kingdom of heaven is like a mustard seed that someone took and sowed in his field; it is the smallest of all seeds, but when it has grown it is the greatest of shrubs and becomes a tree, so that the birds of the air come and make nests in its branches."

MATTHEW 13:31–32

97. BE MYSTERIOUSLY FRUITFUL

Keeping our missionary fervor alive calls for firm trust in the Holy Spirit, for it is He who "helps us in our weakness" (Romans 8:26). But this generous trust has to be nourished, and so we need to invoke the Spirit constantly. He can heal whatever causes us to flag in the missionary endeavor. It is true that this trust in the unseen can cause us to feel disoriented: it is like being plunged into the deep and not knowing what we will find. I myself have frequently experienced this. Yet there is no greater freedom than that of allowing oneself to be guided by the Holy Spirit, renouncing the attempt to plan and control everything to the last detail, and instead letting Him enlighten, guide, and direct us—leading us wherever He wills. The Holy Spirit knows well what is needed in every time and place. This is what it means to be mysteriously fruitful!

Apostolic Exhortation, Evangelii Gaudium, *Chapter Five, I, 280, November 24, 2013*
On the Proclamation of the Gospel in Today's World

✝

We know that all things work together for good for those who love God, who are called according to his purpose.

ROMANS 8:28

98. CARRY ANOTHER'S BURDEN

To live charitably means not looking out for our own interests, but carrying the burdens of the weakest and poorest among us.

Via Twitter @Pontifex, Monday, November 25, 2013

He said also to the one who had invited him, "When you give a luncheon or a dinner, do not invite your friends or your brothers or your relatives or rich neighbors . . . But when you give a banquet, invite the poor, the crippled, the lame, and the blind. And you will be blessed, because they cannot repay you . . ."

LUKE 14:12–14

99. MAKE PEACE POSSIBLE

Allow me to repeat what the Prophet says—listen carefully: "They shall beat their swords into plowshares, and their spears into pruning hooks; nation shall not lift up sword against nation, neither shall they learn war any more." But when will this occur? What a beautiful day it shall be, when weapons are dismantled in order to be transformed into tools for work! What a beautiful day that shall be! And this is possible! Let us bet on hope, on the hope for peace, and it will be possible!

Angelus, Saint Peter's Square, Sunday, December 1, 2013

He shall judge between the nations,
and shall arbitrate for many peoples;
they shall beat their swords into plowshares,
and their spears into pruning hooks;
nation shall not lift a sword against
nation,
neither shall they learn war any more.

ISAIAH 2:4

100. BE HOLY

Holiness doesn't mean doing extraordinary things but doing ordinary things with love and faith.

Via Twitter @Pontifex, Thursday, December 5, 2013

You were taught to put away your former way of life, your old self . . . and to clothe yourselves with the new self, created according to the likeness of God in true righteousness and holiness.

EPHESIANS 4:22,24

101. LOVE TENDERLY

The proof of authentic faith in Christ is self-giving and the spreading of love for our neighbors, especially for those who do not merit it, for the suffering and for the marginalized. . . .

When we draw near with tender love to those in need of care, we bring hope and God's smile to the contradictions of the world. When generous devotion to others becomes the hallmark of our actions, we give way to the Heart of Christ and bask in its warmth, and thus contribute to the coming of God's Kingdom.

Message, Friday, December 6, 2013
For the Twenty-Second World Day of the Sick 2014

We know love by this, that he laid down his life for us—and we ought to lay down our lives for one another. How does God's love abide in anyone who has the world's goods and sees a brother or sister in need and yet refuses to help?

1 JOHN 3:16–17

102. FEED THE HUNGRY

When the Apostles said to Jesus that the people who had come to listen to His words were hungry, He invited them to go and look for food. Being poor themselves, all they found were five loaves and two fish. But with the grace of God, they managed to feed a multitude of people, even managing to collect what was left over and avoiding that it went to waste.

We are in front of a global scandal of around one billion—one *billion*—people who still suffer from hunger today. We cannot look the other way and pretend this does not exist. The food and fish teaches us exactly this: that if there is the will, what we have never ends. On the contrary, it abounds and does not get wasted. Therefore, dear brothers and sisters, I invite you to make space in your heart for this emergency of respecting the God-given rights of everyone to have access to adequate food. We share what we have in Christian charity with those who face numerous obstacles to satisfy such a basic need. At the same time we promote an authentic cooperation with the poor so that, through the fruits of their and our work, they can live a dignified life.

Message, Monday, December 9, 2013
For the Campaign Against Global Hunger, Caritas Internationalis

"... for I was hungry and you gave me food, I was thirsty and
you gave me something to drink ..."

MATTHEW 25:35

103. HEAR GOD'S CALL

The love of God is not generic. God looks with love upon every man and woman, calling them by name.

Via Twitter @Pontifex, Tuesday, December 17, 2013

Then the LORD called, "Samuel! Samuel!"
and he said, "Here I am!"

1 SAMUEL 3:4

104. WALK THE DEMANDING PATH OF LOVE

We Christians believe that in the Church we are all members of a single body, all mutually necessary, because each has been given a grace according to the measure of the gift of Christ, for the common good (cf. Ephesians 4:7, 25; 1 Corinthians 12:7). Christ has come to the world so as to bring us divine grace, that is, the possibility of sharing in His life. This entails weaving a fabric of fraternal relationships marked by reciprocity, forgiveness, and complete self-giving—according to the breadth and the depth of the love of God offered to humanity in the One who, crucified and risen, draws all to Himself: "A new commandment I give to you, that you love one another; even as I have loved you, that you also love one another. By this all will know that you are my disciples, if you have love for one another" (John 13:34–35). This is the Good News that demands from each one a step forward, a perennial exercise of empathy, of listening to the suffering and the hopes of others, even those furthest away from me, and walking the demanding path of that love which knows how to give and spend itself freely for the good of all our brothers and sisters.

Message, Wednesday, January 1, 2014, World Day of Peace

✝

"I give you a new commandment, that you love one another. Just as I have loved you, you should love one another. By this everyone will know that you are my disciples, if you have love for one another."

105. TREAT EACH PERSON AS A BROTHER OR SISTER

In the heart of every man and woman is the desire for a full life, including that irrepressible longing for fraternity which draws us to fellowship with others and enables us to see them not as enemies or rivals, but as brothers and sisters to be accepted and embraced.

Fraternity is an essential human quality, for we are relational beings. A lively awareness of our relatedness helps us to look upon and to treat each person as a true sister or brother. Without fraternity it is impossible to build a just society and a solid and lasting peace. We should remember that fraternity is generally first learned in the family, thanks above all to the responsible and complementary roles of each of its members, particularly the father and the mother. The family is the wellspring of all fraternity, and as such it is the foundation and the first pathway to peace, since, by its vocation, it is meant to spread its love to the world around it.

Message, Wednesday, January 1, 2014
World Day of Peace

All who believed were together and had all things in common; they
would sell their possessions and goods and distribute the proceeds to all,
as any had need.

Acts 2:44-45

106. SET OUT ON THE PATH OF JUSTICE AND PEACE

. . . may the Lord help us all to set out more decisively on the path of justice and peace. And let us begin at home! Justice and peace at home, among ourselves. It begins at home and then goes out to all humanity. But we have to begin at home. May the Holy Spirit act in hearts, may He melt obstacles and hardness and grant that we may be moved before the weakness of the Baby Jesus. Peace, in fact, requires the strength of meekness, the nonviolent strength of truth and love.

Angelus, Saint Peter's Square, Wednesday, January 1, 2014
Solemnity of Mary, Mother of God, Forty-Seventh World Day of Peace

✝

He has told you, O mortal, what is good;
and what does the LORD require of you
but to do justice, and to love kindness,
and to walk humbly with your God?

MICAH 6:8

107. SET A PLACE AT
YOUR TABLE

Let us leave a spare place at our table: a place for those who lack the basics, who are alone.

Via Twitter @Pontifex, Tuesday, January 7, 2014

"For you always have the poor with you, and you can show kindness to
them whenever you wish . . ."

MARK 14:7

108. FOLLOW THE WAY OF CHARITY

Sharing is the true way to love. Jesus does not dissociate Himself from us, He considers us brothers and sisters and He shares with us. And so He makes us sons and daughters, together with Him, of God the Father. This is the revelation and source of true love. And this is the great time of mercy! Does it not seem to you that in our own time extra fraternal sharing and love is needed? Does it not seem to you that we all need extra charity? Not the sort that is content with extemporaneous help which does not involve or stake anything, but that charity that shares, that takes on the hardship and suffering of a brother. What flavor life acquires when we allow ourselves to be inundated by God's love!

Angelus, Saint Peter's Square, Sunday, January 12, 2014
Feast of the Baptism of the Lord

✝

"I give you a new commandment, that you love one another. Just as I have loved you, you also should love one another. By this everyone will know that you are my disciples, if you have love for one another."

JOHN 13:34–35

109. OPEN THE DOOR

The Lord is knocking at the door of our hearts. Have we put a sign on the door saying: "Do not disturb"?

Via Twitter @Pontifex, Monday, January 13, 2014

†

"Ask, and it will be given you; search, and you will find;
knock, and the door will be opened for you."

MATTHEW 7:7

110. BE DISCIPLES

What does it mean . . . for us today, to be disciples of Jesus, the Lamb of God? It means replacing malice with innocence, replacing power with love, replacing pride with humility, replacing status with service. It is good work! We Christians must do this: replace malice with innocence, replace power with love, replace pride with humility, replace status with service. . . . It means not assuming closed attitudes, but rather proposing the Gospel to everyone, bearing witness by our lives that following Jesus makes us freer and more joyous.

Angelus, Saint Peter's Square, Sunday, January 19, 2014

†

"Whoever serves me must follow me, and where I am, there will my servant be also. Whoever serves me, the Father will honor."

John 12:26

111. TRUST IN THE LORD

Many times we trust a doctor: it is good, because the doctor is there to cure us. We trust in a person: brothers and sisters can help us. It is good to have this human trust among ourselves. But we forget about trust in the Lord: this is the key to success in life. Trust in the Lord, let us trust in the Lord! "Lord, look at my life: I'm in the dark, I have this struggle, I have this sin . . ." Everything we have: "Look at this: I trust in you!" And this is a risk we must take: to trust in Him, and He never disappoints. Never, never!

Homily, Sunday, January 19, 2014
Pastoral Visit to the Roman Parish Sacred Heart of Jesus in Castro Pretorio

Blessed are those who trust in the LORD,
whose trust is the LORD.

JEREMIAH 17:7

112. REMAIN FAITHFUL

In proclaiming the Beatitudes, Jesus asks us to follow Him and to travel with Him along the path of love, the path that alone leads to eternal life. It is not an easy journey, yet the Lord promises us His grace and He never abandons us. We face so many challenges in life: poverty, distress, humiliation, the struggle for justice, persecutions, the difficulty of daily conversion, the effort to remain faithful to our call to holiness, and many others. But if we open the door to Jesus and allow Him to be part of our lives, if we share our joys and sorrows with Him, then we will experience the peace and joy that only God, who is infinite love, can give.

Message, Tuesday, January 21, 2014
For the Twenty-Ninth World Youth Day 2014

†

"Blessed are the poor in spirit, for theirs is the kingdom of heaven."

Matthew 5:3

113. BE BLESSED . . . THINK BIG!

What does it mean to be "blessed" (*makarioi* in Greek)? To be blessed means to be happy. Tell me: Do you really want to be happy? In an age when we are constantly being enticed by vain and empty illusions of happiness, we risk settling for less and "thinking small" when it comes to the meaning of life. Think big instead! Open your hearts!

Message, Tuesday, January 21, 2014
For the Twenty-Ninth World Youth Day 2014

✝

I will exult and rejoice in your steadfast love . . .

PSALM 31:7

114. HAVE THE COURAGE TO
BE TRULY HAPPY

If you are really open to the deepest aspirations of your hearts, you will realize that you possess an unquenchable thirst for happiness, and this will allow you to expose and reject the "low cost" offers and approaches all around you. When we look only for success, pleasure and possessions, and we turn these into idols, we may well have moments of exhilaration, an illusory sense of satisfaction, but ultimately we become enslaved, never satisfied, always looking for more. It is a tragic thing to see a young person who "has everything," but is weary and weak. . . .

Have the courage to swim against the tide. Have the courage to be truly happy! Say no to an ephemeral, superficial and throwaway culture—a culture that assumes that you are incapable of taking on responsibility and facing the great challenges of life!

Message, Tuesday, January 21, 2014
For the Twenty-Ninth World Youth Day 2014

✝

I write to you . . . because you are strong
and the word of God abides in you,
and you have overcome the evil one.

1 JOHN 2:14

115. LEARN FROM PEOPLE WHO ARE POOR

The poor are not just people to whom we can give something. They have *much to offer us and to teach us.* How much we have to learn from the wisdom of the poor! . . . In a very real way, the poor are our teachers. They show us that people's value is not measured by their possessions or how much money they have in the bank. A poor person, a person lacking material possessions, always maintains his or her dignity. The poor can teach us much about humility and trust in God.

Message, Tuesday, January 21, 2014
For the Twenty-Ninth World Youth Day 2014

✝

He looked up and saw rich people putting their gifts into the treasury; he also saw a poor widow put in two small copper coins. He said, "Truly I tell you, this poor widow has put in more than all of them; for all of them have contributed out of their abundance, but she out of her poverty has put in all she had to live on."

LUKE 21:1–4

116. BE BRAVE,
GO WITH THE LORD!

The Lord passes through the paths of our daily life. Even today at this moment, here, the Lord is passing through the square. He is calling us to go with Him, to work with Him for the Kingdom of God, in the "Galilee" of our times. May each one of you think: the Lord is passing by today, the Lord is watching me, He is looking at me! What is the Lord saying to me? And if one of you feels that the Lord says to you "follow me," be brave, go with the Lord. The Lord never disappoints. Feel in your heart if the Lord is calling you to follow Him. Let's let His gaze rest on us, hear His voice, and follow Him! "That the joy of the Gospel may reach to the ends of the earth, illuminating even the fringes of our world"

Apostolic Exhortation, Evangelii Gaudium, Chapter Five, II, 288,
Angelus, Saint Peter's Square, Sunday, January 26, 2014

†

As Jesus passed along the Sea of Galilee, he saw Simon and his brother
Andrew casting a net into the sea—for they were fishermen. And Jesus
said to them, "Follow me and I will make you fish for people." And
immediately they left their nets and followed him.

MARK 1:16–18

117. BE AMAZED!

Dear young people, let us not be satisfied with a mediocre life. Be amazed by what is true and beautiful, what is of God!

Via Twitter @Pontifex, Monday, January 27, 2014

✝

God saw everything that he had made, and indeed, it was very good.
And there was evening and there was morning, the sixth day.

GENESIS 1:31

118. BRING LIGHT TO THE WORLD

This mission of giving light to the world is so beautiful! We have this mission, and it is beautiful! It is also beautiful to keep the light we have received from Jesus, protecting it and safeguarding it. The Christian should be a luminous person—one who brings light, who always gives off light! A light that is not his, but a gift from God, a gift from Jesus. We carry this light. If a Christian extinguishes this light, his life has no meaning: he is a Christian by name only, who does not carry light—his life has no meaning. I would like to ask you now, how do you want to live? As a lamp that is burning or one that is not? Burning or not? How would you like to live? [The people respond: Burning!] As burning lamps! It is truly God who gives us this light and we must give it to others. Shining lamps! This is the Christian vocation.

Angelus, Saint Peter's Square, Sunday, February 9, 2014

✝

"You are the light of the world. A city built on a hill cannot be hid. No one after lighting a lamp puts it under the bushel basket, but on the lampstand, and it gives light to all in the house. In the same way, let your light shine before others, so that they may see your good works and give glory to your Father in heaven."

MATTHEW 5:14–16

119. WALK WITH JOY

Joy is the way of the Christian. The Christian cannot walk without joy. One cannot walk as a lamb without joy. The Christian must preserve this attitude always, even amid problems, in moments of difficulty, even amid his own mistakes and sins, because Jesus always forgives and helps us, and there is always joy. . . . The Christian is one who never stands still, but always moves forward beyond difficulties. And he does this with strength and joy.

Morning Meditation, Chapel of the Domus Sanctae Marthae, Friday, February 14, 2014

✝

You show me the path of life.
In your presence there is fullness of joy;
in your right hand are pleasures forevermore.

PSALM 16:11

120. AVOID GOSSIP

When we say that a person has the tongue of a snake, what does that mean? That their words kill! Not only is it wrong to take the life of another, but it is also wrong to bestow the poison of anger upon him, strike him with slander, and speak ill of him.

This brings us to gossip: gossip can also kill, because it kills the reputation of the person! It is so terrible to gossip! At first it may seem like a nice thing, even amusing, like enjoying a candy. But in the end, it fills the heart with bitterness, and even poisons us. What I am telling you is true, I am convinced that if each one of us decided to avoid gossiping, we would eventually become holy! What a beautiful path that is! Do we want to become holy? Yes or no? [The people: Yes!] Do we want to be attached to the habit of gossip? Yes or no? [The people: No!] So we agree then: no gossiping! Jesus offers the perfection of love to those who follow Him: love is the only measure that has no measure, to move past judgments.

Angelus, Saint Peter's Square, Sunday, February 16, 2014

"So when you are offering your gift at the altar, if you remember that
your brother or sister has something against you, leave your gift there
before the altar and go; first be reconciled to your brother or sister, and
then come and offer your gift."

MATTHEW 5:23–24

121. BE HONEST WITH YOURSELF

Being honest with yourself is not easy! Because we always try to cover it up when we see something wrong inside, no? So that it doesn't come out, don't we? What is in our heart: is it love? Let us think: do I love my parents, my children, my wife, my husband, people in the neighborhood, the sick? . . . Do I love? Is there hate? Do I hate someone? Often we find hatred, don't we? "I love everyone except for this one, this one, and that one!" That's hatred, isn't it? What is in my heart— forgiveness? Is there an attitude of forgiveness for those who have offended me, or is there an attitude of revenge—"he will pay for it!" We must ask ourselves what is within, because what is inside comes out and harms, if it is evil. And if it is good, it comes out and does good. And it is so beautiful to tell ourselves the truth, and feel ashamed when we are in a situation that is not what God wants, it is not good—when my heart feels hatred, revenge, so many situations are sinful. How is my heart?

Homily, Sunday, February 16, 2014
Pastoral Visit to the Roman Parish San Tommaso Apostolo

✝

"Blessed are the pure in heart, for they will see God."

MATTHEW 5:8

122. SEEK GOD'S KINGDOM, TOGETHER

You cannot serve two masters: God and wealth. As long as everyone seeks to accumulate for themselves, there will never be justice. We must take heed of this! As long as everyone seeks to accumulate for themselves, there will be no justice. Instead, by entrusting ourselves to God's providence, and seeking His Kingdom together, no one will lack the necessary means to live with dignity.

Angelus, Saint Peter's Square, Sunday, March 2, 2014

†

"But strive for the kingdom of God and his righteousness, and all these things will be given to you as well."

MATTHEW 6:33

123. SHARE WITH OTHERS

Jesus frequently warned the rich, because they greatly risk placing their security in the goods of this world—and security, the final security, is in God. In a heart possessed by wealth, there isn't much room for faith: everything is involved with wealth, there is no room for faith. If, however, one gives God His rightful place, that is first place, then His love leads one to share even one's wealth, to set it at the service of projects of solidarity and development . . . If each of us accumulates not for ourselves alone but for the service of others, in this case, in this act of solidarity, the Providence of God is made visible. If, however, one accumulates only for oneself, what will happen when one is called by God? No one can take his riches with him, because—as you know—the shroud has no pockets! It is better to share, for we can take with us to Heaven only what we have shared with others.

Angelus, Saint Peter's Square, Sunday, March 2, 2014

"'It is more blessed to give than to receive.'"

ACTS 20:35

124. DIVE INTO THE SEA OF PRAYER

Prayer is the strength of the Christian and of every person who believes. In the weakness and frailty of our lives, we can turn to God with the confidence of children and enter into communion with Him. In the face of so many wounds that hurt us and could harden our hearts, we are called to dive into the sea of prayer, which is the sea of God's boundless love, to taste His tenderness.

Homily, Basilica of Santa Sabina, Wednesday, March 5, 2014
Holy Mass, Blessing and Imposition of the Ashes

"So I tell you, whatever you ask for in prayer,
believe that you have received it, and it will be yours."

MARK 11:24

125. BE GRATEFUL

Gratuitousness should be one of the characteristics of the Christian who, aware of having received everything from God gratuitously—that is, without any merit of his own—learns to give to others freely. Today gratuitousness is often not part of daily life where everything is bought and sold. Everything is calculated and measured. Almsgiving helps us to experience giving freely, which leads to freedom from the obsession of possessing, from the fear of losing what we have, from the sadness of one who does not wish to share his wealth with others.

Homily, Basilica of Santa Sabina, Wednesday, March 5, 2014
Holy Mass, Blessing and Imposition of the Ashes

Those who are generous are blessed,
for they share their bread with the poor.

PSALM 22:9

Appendix

THEME	REFLECTION TITLE	REFLECTION NUMBER
beauty	Make a world of goodness, beauty, and truth.	52
	Be amazed!	117
blessedness	Be blessed . . . think big!	113
blessings	Remember.	11
	Let God's love lift you up and lead you on.	12
charity	Love someone well today.	18
	Share your gifts.	28
	Be courageous.	61
	Follow the way of charity.	108

THEME	REFLECTION TITLE	REFLECTION NUMBER
common good	Pray for leaders.	59
	Walk the demanding path of love.	104
compassion	Decide to be a Good Samaritan.	27
consolation	Experience the consolation of God.	31
control	Be surprised by God.	81
courage	Be faithful.	21
	Pray bravely.	29
	Be courageous.	61
	Put out into the deep!	67
	Take a few steps outside of yourself.	68
	Have the courage to be truly happy.	114

THEME	REFLECTION TITLE	REFLECTION NUMBER
creation	Care for creation.	25
	Respect creation.	78
dialogue	Start the beautiful adventure of dialogue.	48
discernment	Ask for the wisdom of discernment.	53
discipleship	Go and bring Christ.	40
	Bring the love of Jesus to others.	93
	Be disciples.	110
	Be brave, go with the Lord!	116
diversity	Start the beautiful adventure of dialogue.	48
doubt	Find the Word of God in the history of each day.	80
ecumenism	Start the beautiful adventure of dialogue.	48

THEME	REFLECTION TITLE	REFLECTION NUMBER
elderly	Honor the strength of the young and the wisdom of the elderly.	34
	Honor your parents and the elderly.	75
	Keep memory alive.	89
evil	Build a new world.	41
faith	Be an everyday saint.	15
	Put on faith, hope, and love.	38
	Have an action plan.	39
	Enter through Jesus's door.	49
	Awaken the memory of God in your life.	74
	Reach for the Lord's outstretched hand.	82
	Love tenderly.	101
	Be holy.	100

THEME	REFLECTION TITLE	REFLECTION NUMBER
faithfulness	Trust that God waits for you.	13
	Be faithful.	21
	Choose to follow Jesus.	45
	Choose God as the criterion for your life.	47
	Keep Jesus at the center.	54
	Be amazed by God's love and mercy.	87
	Be mysteriously fruitful.	97
	Remain faithful.	112
family	Be protectors of God's gifts.	6
	Say "thank you."	83
	Treat each person as a brother or sister.	105
	Set out on the path of justice and peace.	106

THEME	REFLECTION TITLE	REFLECTION NUMBER
forgiveness	Ponder the patience God has for you.	2
	Never tire of asking for forgiveness.	4
	Never give up.	10
	Put your heart into works of mercy.	64
	Encounter the Lord.	91
fraternity	Treat each person as a brother or sister.	105
freedom	Choose the good of all.	56
generosity	Love tenderly.	101
	Feed the hungry.	102
	Set a place at your table.	107
	Share with others.	123
God, choose	Choose God as the criterion for your life.	47
God, flee from	Resist the temptation to run away from God.	79

THEME	REFLECTION TITLE	REFLECTION NUMBER
God, loved by	Experience the consolation of God.	31
God's goodness	Imitate God.	23
God's image	Help one person have a better life.	95
God's love	Go forward, with love.	43
	Be amazed by God's love and mercy.	87
	Hear God's call.	103
God's presence	Seek God in every human life.	76
God's Word	Find the Word of God in the history of each day.	80
God's world	Choose the good of all.	56
goodness	Choose goodness, truth, and justice.	46
	Make a world of goodness, beauty, and truth.	52
	Choose the good of all.	56
	Spread goodness.	90

THEME	REFLECTION TITLE	REFLECTION NUMBER
gossip	Avoid gossip.	120
gratitude	Say "thank you."	83
	Be grateful.	125
happiness	Be blessed . . . think big!	113
	Have the courage to be truly happy.	114
harmony	Choose the good of all.	56
hatred	Build a new world.	41
holiness	Be an everyday saint.	15
	Walk with determination.	20
	Walk the way of holiness.	86
	Help one person have a better life.	95
	Be holy.	100
Holy Spirit	Be mysteriously fruitful.	97
honesty	Be honest with yourself.	121

THEME	REFLECTION TITLE	REFLECTION NUMBER
hope	Open up a horizon of hope.	5
	Let Jesus carry you.	8
	Never give up.	10
	Be surprised by God's love.	35
	Be lights of hope!	37
	Put on faith, hope, and love.	38
	Believe in the victory of love.	44
	Have hope.	66
	Make peace possible.	99
	Go forward on the path of hope.	88
	Believe that the Kingdom of God is already present.	96
hospitality	Set a place at your table.	107

THEME	REFLECTION TITLE	REFLECTION NUMBER
humility	Seek humility, service, and love.	24
	Give yourself to another with love.	63
	Put your heart into works of mercy.	64
	Serve humbly.	65
	Let God write your history.	70
	Worship God and serve others.	77
	Find the Word of God in the history of each day.	80
hunger	Feed the hungry.	102
hypocrisy	Take responsibility.	32
inclusiveness	Be leavening.	71
indifference	Take responsibility.	32
idolatry, idols	Beware of the trap of idolatry.	60
	Center your life on the Lord.	85
Jesus	Bring the love of Jesus to others.	93

THEME	REFLECTION TITLE	REFLECTION NUMBER
Jesus, following	Let Jesus carry you.	8
	Recognize the voice of Jesus.	17
	Choose to follow Jesus.	45
	Let God write your history.	70
Jesus's suffering	Accept your cross.	73
Jesus, the Cross	Accept your cross.	73
journey	Journey in the presence of the Lord.	1
	Go forward with Jesus.	69
	Reach for the Lord's outstretched hand.	82
joy	Let Jesus carry you.	8
	Spread joy.	36
	Open your heart.	94
	Be brave, go with the Lord!	116
	Walk with joy.	119

THEME	REFLECTION TITLE	REFLECTION NUMBER
justice	Keep alive the thirst for God.	7
	Choose goodness, truth, and justice.	46
	Be Christian by the truth.	50
	Feed the hungry.	102
	Set out on the path of justice and peace.	106
	Seek God's Kingdom, together.	122
Kingdom of God	Believe that the Kingdom of God is already present.	96
	Love tenderly.	101
	Be brave, go with the Lord!	116
	Seek God's Kingdom, together.	122
leadership	Pray for leaders.	59
letting go	Be surprised by God.	81

THEME	REFLECTION TITLE	REFLECTION NUMBER
life, the Christian life, Christian living	Walk with determination.	20
	Be a full-time Christian.	30
	Be Christian by the truth.	50
	Keep Jesus at the center.	54
	Be merciful.	58
	Put out into the deep!	67
	Reach for the Lord's outstretched hand.	82
	Walk the way of holiness.	86
	Carry another's burden.	98
	Remain faithful.	112
	Have the courage to be truly happy.	114
	Walk with joy.	119
	Avoid gossip.	120

THEME	REFLECTION TITLE	REFLECTION NUMBER
life, everyday living	Be an everyday saint.	15
	Love someone well today.	18
	Show a sign of love.	19
	Say "yes" to love.	26
	Be a full-time Christian.	30
	Put on faith, hope, and love.	38
	Have an action plan.	39
	Enter through Jesus's door.	49
	Reach for the Lord's outstretched hand.	82
	Encounter the Lord.	91
	Be holy.	100

THEME	REFLECTION TITLE	REFLECTION NUMBER
life, family life	Say "thank you."	83
life, fullness of	Be amazed by God's love and mercy.	87
	Go forward on the path of hope.	88
life, new	Never give up.	10
	Say "yes" to love.	26
light	Be lights of hope!	37
	Ask for the wisdom of discernment.	53
	Bring light to the world.	118
listening	Be leavening.	71
	Talk to Jesus.	72

THEME	REFLECTION TITLE	REFLECTION NUMBER
love	Answer adversity with love.	14
	Love someone well today.	18
	Imitate God.	23
	Say "yes" to love.	26
	Be a full-time Christian.	30
	Put on faith, hope, and love.	38
	Go and bring Christ.	40
	Encounter Jesus.	42
	Go forward, with love.	43
	Believe in the victory of love.	44
	Seek the good of others, ceaselessly.	51
	Walk the path of peace.	55
	Give yourself to another with love.	63
	Put your heart into works of mercy.	64
	Take a step forward in love.	92

THEME	REFLECTION TITLE	REFLECTION NUMBER
love (cont.)	Bring the love of Jesus to others.	93
	Open your heart.	94
	Help one person have a better life.	95
	Carry another's burden.	98
	Love tenderly.	101
	Hear God's call.	103
	Walk the demanding path of love.	104
	Set a place at your table.	107
	Follow the way of charity.	108
	Dive into the sea of prayer.	124
materialism	Center your life on the Lord.	85
meekness	Worship God and serve others.	77
memory	Remember.	11
	Awaken the memory of God in your life.	74
	Keep memory alive.	89

APPENDIX

THEME	REFLECTION TITLE	REFLECTION NUMBER
mercy	Ponder the patience God has for you.	2
	Be a person of mercy.	3
	Never tire of asking for forgiveness.	4
	Let God's love lift you up and lead you on.	12
	Go and bring Christ.	40
	Be merciful.	58
	Put your heart into works of mercy.	64
	Reach for the Lord's outstretched hand.	82
	Encounter the Lord.	91
mission	Bring light to the world.	118
money	Beware of the trap of idolatry.	60
	Center your life on the Lord.	85

THEME	REFLECTION TITLE	REFLECTION NUMBER
openness	Be open to God's surprises.	22
	Enter through Jesus's door.	49
	Take a few steps outside of yourself.	68
	Open your heart.	94
	Open the door.	109
	Remain faithful.	112
	Learn from people who are poor.	115
outreach	Go and bring Christ.	40
	Go forward, with love.	43
	Take a few steps outside of yourself.	68
	Be leavening.	71
parents	Honor your parents and the elderly.	75
patience	Ponder the patience God has for you.	2
	Go forward on the path of hope.	88

THEME	REFLECTION TITLE	REFLECTION NUMBER
peace	Walk the path of peace.	55
	Respect creation.	78
	Make peace possible.	99
	Set out on the path of justice and peace.	106
poor	Learn from people who are poor.	115
prayer	Pray bravely.	29
	Knock at the door of God's heart.	62
	Go forward with Jesus.	69
	Talk to Jesus.	72
	Pray always.	84
	Walk the way of holiness.	86
	Take a step forward in love.	92
	Dive into the sea of prayer.	124

THEME	REFLECTION TITLE	REFLECTION NUMBER
presence	Answer adversity with love.	14
	Be lights of hope!	37
priorities	Encounter Jesus.	42
	Beware of the trap of idolatry.	60
reconciliation	Walk the path of peace.	55
respect	Be faithful.	21
	Respect creation.	78
risk	Talk to Jesus.	72
saints	Go forward with Jesus.	69
	Walk the way of holiness.	86
self-examination	Be honest with yourself.	121
selfishness	Build a new world.	41

THEME	REFLECTION TITLE	REFLECTION NUMBER
service	Serve others.	9
	Seek humility, service, and love.	24
	Decide to be a Good Samaritan.	27
	Have an action plan.	39
	Serve humbly.	65
	Worship God and serve others.	77
	Feed the hungry.	102
	Be disciples.	110
sin	Serve humbly.	65
solidarity	Give yourself to another with love.	63
	Take a few steps outside of yourself.	68
	Share with others.	123

THEME	REFLECTION TITLE	REFLECTION NUMBER
stewardship	Be protectors of God's gifts.	6
	Care for creation.	25
	Be grateful.	125
suffering	Take responsibility.	32
	Believe in the victory of love.	44
	Contemplate Jesus suffering.	57
	Accept your cross.	73
surprise	Be surprised by God's love.	35
	Be surprised by God.	81
temptation	Resist the temptation to run away from God.	79
tenderness	Love tenderly.	101
	Dive into the sea of prayer.	124

THEME	REFLECTION TITLE	REFLECTION NUMBER
trust	Trust that God waits for you.	13
	Put out into the deep!	67
	Seek God in every human life.	76
	Be surprised by God.	81
	Be mysteriously fruitful.	97
	Trust in the Lord.	111
	Learn from people who are poor.	115
truth	Answer adversity with love.	14
	Choose goodness, truth, and justice.	46
	Be Christian by the truth.	50
	Make a world of goodness, beauty, and truth.	52
	Ask for the wisdom of discernment.	53
	Spread goodness.	90
violence	Build a new world.	41

THEME	REFLECTION TITLE	REFLECTION NUMBER
vocation	Bring light to the world.	118
wealth	Share with others.	123
wisdom	Honor the strength of the young and the wisdom of the elderly.	34
	Ask for the wisdom of discernment.	53
	Learn from people who are poor.	115
witness	Preach with your life.	16
	Experience the consolation of God.	31
	Be Christian by the truth.	50
youth	Rise to the promise found in young people.	33
	Honor the strength of the young and the wisdom of the elderly.	34
	Build a new world.	41
	Keep memory alive.	89
	Be amazed!	117

Sources

1. http://www.vatican.va/holy_father/francesco/homilies/2013/documents/papa
   -francesco_20130314_omelia-cardinali_en.html

2. http://www.vatican.va/holy_father/francesco/angelus/2013/documents/papa-francesco
   _angelus_20130317_en.html

3. http://www.vatican.va/holy_father/francesco/homilies/2013/documents/papa
   -francesco_20130317_omelia-santa-anna_en.html

4. http://www.vatican.va/holy_father/francesco/homilies/2013/documents/papa
   -francesco_20130317_omelia-santa-anna_en.html

5. http://www.vatican.va/holy_father/francesco/homilies/2013/documents/papa
   -francesco_20130319_omelia-inizio-pontificato_en.html

6. http://www.vatican.va/holy_father/francesco/homilies/2013/documents/papa
   -francesco_20130319_omelia-inizio-pontificato_en.html

7. http://www.vatican.va/holy_father/francesco/speeches/2013/march/documents/papa
   -francesco_20130320_delegati-fraterni_en.html

8. http://www.vatican.va/holy_father/francesco/homilies/2013/documents/papa
   -francesco_20130324_palme_en.html

9. http://www.vatican.va/holy_father/francesco/homilies/2013/documents/papa
-francesco_20130328_coena-domini_en.html

10. http://www.vatican.va/holy_father/francesco/homilies/2013/documents/papa
-francesco_20130330_veglia-pasquale_en.html

11. http://www.vatican.va/holy_father/francesco/homilies/2013/documents/papa
-francesco_20130330_veglia-pasquale_en.html

12. http://www.vatican.va/holy_father/francesco/homilies/2013/documents/papa
-francesco_20130407_omelia-possesso-cattedra-laterano_en.html

13. http://www.vatican.va/holy_father/francesco/homilies/2013/documents/papa
-francesco_20130407_omelia-possesso-cattedra-laterano_en.html

14. http://www.vatican.va/holy_father/francesco/angelus/2013/documents/papa-francesco
_regina-coeli_20130414_en.html

15. http://www.vatican.va/holy_father/francesco/homilies/2013/documents/papa
-francesco_20130414_omelia-basilica-san-paolo_en.html

16. http://www.vatican.va/holy_father/francesco/homilies/2013/documents/papa
-francesco_20130414_omelia-basilica-san-paolo_en.html

17. http://www.vatican.va/holy_father/francesco/angelus/2013/documents/papa-francesco
_regina-coeli_20130421_en.html

18. https://twitter.com/Pontifex

19. http://www.vatican.va/holy_father/francesco/homilies/2013/documents/papa
-francesco_20130428_omelia-cresime_en.html

20. https://twitter.com/Pontifex

21. http://www.vatican.va/holy_father/francesco/homilies/2013/documents/papa
-francesco_20130512_omelia-canonizzazioni_en.html

22. http://www.vatican.va/holy_father/francesco/homilies/2013/documents/papa
-francesco_20130519_omelia-pentecoste_en.html

23. http://www.vatican.va/holy_father/francesco/speeches/2013/may/documents/papa
-francesco_20130524_migranti-itineranti_en.html

24. https://twitter.com/Pontifex

25. https://twitter.com/Pontifex

26. http://www.vatican.va/holy_father/francesco/homilies/2013/documents/papa
-francesco_20130616_omelia-evangelium-vitae_en.html

27. http://www.vatican.va/holy_father/francesco/speeches/2013/june/documents/papa
-francesco_20130620_38-sessione-fao_en.html

28. https://twitter.com/Pontifex

29. http://www.vatican.va/holy_father/francesco/cotidie/2013/en/papa-francesco
-cotidie_20130701_praying-bravely_en.html

30. http://www.vatican.va/holy_father/francesco/cotidie/2013/en/papa-francesco
-cotidie_20130706_renewal-without-fear_en.html (by *L'Osservatore Romano*, weekly
ed. in English, n. 27, 17 July 2013)

31. http://www.vatican.va/holy_father/francesco/homilies/2013/documents/papa
-francesco_20130707_omelia-seminaristi-novizie_en.html

32. http://www.vatican.va/holy_father/francesco/homilies/2013/documents/papa
-francesco_20130708_omelia-lampedusa_en.html

33. http://www.vatican.va/holy_father/francesco/speeches/2013/july/documents/papa
-francesco_20130722_gmg-cerimonia-benvenuto-rio_en.html

34. http://www.vatican.va/holy_father/francesco/speeches/2013/july/documents/papa
-francesco_20130722_gmg-intervista-volo-rio_en.html

35. http://www.vatican.va/holy_father/francesco/homilies/2013/documents/papa
-francesco_20130724_gmg-omelia-aparecida_en.html

36. http://www.vatican.va/holy_father/francesco/homilies/2013/documents/papa
-francesco_20130724_gmg-omelia-aparecida_en.html

37. http://www.vatican.va/holy_father/francesco/homilies/2013/documents/papa
-francesco_20130724_gmg-omelia-aparecida_en.html

38. http://www.vatican.va/holy_father/francesco/speeches/2013/july/documents/papa
-francesco_20130725_gmg-giovani-rio_en.html#

39. http://www.vatican.va/holy_father/francesco/speeches/2013/july/documents/papa
-francesco_20130725_gmg-argentini-rio_en.html

40. http://www.vatican.va/holy_father/francesco/homilies/2013/documents/papa
-francesco_20130728_celebrazione-xxviii-gmg_en.html

41. http://www.vatican.va/holy_father/francesco/homilies/2013/documents/papa
-francesco_20130728_celebrazione-xxviii-gmg_en.html

42. http://www.vatican.va/holy_father/francesco/angelus/2013/documents/papa-francesco
_angelus_20130811_en.html

43. http://www.vatican.va/holy_father/francesco/angelus/2013/documents/papa-francesco
_angelus_20130811_en.html

44. http://www.vatican.va/holy_father/francesco/homilies/2013/documents/papa
-francesco_20130815_omelia-assunzione_en.html

45. http://www.vatican.va/holy_father/francesco/angelus/2013/documents/papa-francesco
_angelus_20130818_en.html

46. http://www.vatican.va/holy_father/francesco/angelus/2013/documents/papa-francesco
_angelus_20130818_en.html

47. http://www.vatican.va/holy_father/francesco/angelus/2013/documents/papa-francesco
_angelus_20130818_en.html

48. http://www.vatican.va/holy_father/francesco/speeches/2013/august/documents/papa
-francesco_20130821_collegio-saitama-giappone_en.html

49. http://www.vatican.va/holy_father/francesco/angelus/2013/documents/papa-francesco_angelus_20130825_en.html

50. http://www.vatican.va/holy_father/francesco/angelus/2013/documents/papa-francesco_angelus_20130825_en.html

51. http://www.vatican.va/holy_father/francesco/homilies/2013/documents/papa-francesco_20130828_capitolo-sant-agostino_en.html

52. http://www.vatican.va/holy_father/francesco/speeches/2013/august/documents/papa-francesco_20130828_giovani-piacenza-bobbio_en.html

53. http://www.vatican.va/holy_father/francesco/cotidie/2013/en/papa-francesco-cotidie_20130903_humble-light_en.html by *L'Osservatore Romano*, weekly ed. in English, n. 37, 11 September 2013

54. http://www.vatican.va/holy_father/francesco/cotidie/2013/en/papa-francesco-cotidie_20130907_no-christian-without-jesus_en.html by *L'Osservatore Romano*, weekly ed. in English, n. 37, 11 September 2013

55. http://www.vatican.va/holy_father/francesco/homilies/2013/documents/papa-francesco_20130907_veglia-pace_en.html

56. http://www.vatican.va/holy_father/francesco/homilies/2013/documents/papa-francesco_20130907_veglia-pace_en.html

57. http://www.vatican.va/holy_father/francesco/cotidie/2013/en/papa-francesco-cotidie_20130912_meek-suffering_en.html by *L'Osservatore Romano*, weekly ed. in English, n. 38, 18 September 2013

58. http://www.vatican.va/holy_father/francesco/angelus/2013/documents/papa-francesco_angelus_20130915_en.html

59. http://www.vatican.va/holy_father/francesco/cotidie/2013/en/papa-francesco-cotidie_20130916_politicians_en.html by *L'Osservatore Romano*, weekly ed. in English, n. 39, 25 September 2013

60. http://www.vatican.va/holy_father/francesco/cotidie/2013/en/papa-francesco
-cotidie_20130920_power-money_en.html by *L'Osservatore Romano*, weekly ed. in
English, n. 39, 25 September 2013

61. https://twitter.com/Pontifex

62. http://www.vatican.va/holy_father/francesco/homilies/2013/documents/papa
-francesco_20130922_bonaria-cagliari_en.html

63. http://www.vatican.va/holy_father/francesco/speeches/2013/september/documents/papa
-francesco_20130922_emarginati-cagliari_en.html#

64. http://www.vatican.va/holy_father/francesco/speeches/2013/september/documents/papa
-francesco_20130922_emarginati-cagliari_en.html#

65. http://www.vatican.va/holy_father/francesco/speeches/2013/september/documents/papa
-francesco_20130922_emarginati-cagliari_en.html#

66. http://www.vatican.va/holy_father/francesco/speeches/2013/september/documents/papa
-francesco_20130922_giovani-cagliari_en.html#

67. http://www.vatican.va/holy_father/francesco/speeches/2013/september/documents/papa
-francesco_20130922_giovani-cagliari_en.html#

68. http://www.vatican.va/holy_father/francesco/speeches/2013/september/documents/papa
-francesco_20130922_giovani-cagliari_en.html#

69. http://www.vatican.va/holy_father/francesco/speeches/2013/september/documents/papa
-francesco_20130922_giovani-cagliari_en.html#

70. http://www.vatican.va/holy_father/francesco/cotidie/2013/en/papa-francesco
-cotidie_20130924_travelling-companion_en.html by *L'Osservatore Romano*, weekly
ed. in English, n. 40, 2 October 2013

71. http://www.news.va/en/news/pope-shares-his-vision-reform-of-church-with-itali

72. http://www.vatican.va/holy_father/francesco/cotidie/2013/en/papa-francesco
-cotidie_20130926_knowing-jesus_en.html by *L'Osservatore Romano*, weekly ed. in
English, n. 40, 2 October 2013

73. http://www.vatican.va/holy_father/francesco/cotidie/2013/en/papa-francesco
-cotidie_20130928_fear-cross_en.html by *L'Osservatore Romano*, weekly ed. in
English, n. 41, 9 October 2013

74. http://www.vatican.va/holy_father/francesco/homilies/2013/documents/papa
-francesco_20130929_giornata-catechisti_en.html

75. http://www.vatican.va/holy_father/francesco/cotidie/2013/en/papa-francesco
-cotidie_20130930_air-church_en.html by *L'Osservatore Romano*, weekly ed. in
English, n. 41, 9 October 2013

76. http://www.americamagazine.org/pope-interview; also see http://w2.vatican.va/content/
francesco/en/speeches/2013/september/documents/papa-francesco_20130921_intervista
-spadaro.html

77. http://www.vatican.va/holy_father/francesco/cotidie/2013/en/papa-francesco
-cotidie_20131001_humility-gospel_en.html by *L'Osservatore Romano*, weekly ed. in
English, n. 41, 9 October 2013

78. http://www.vatican.va/holy_father/francesco/homilies/2013/documents/papa
-francesco_20131004_omelia-visita-assisi_en.html#

79. http://www.vatican.va/holy_father/francesco/cotidie/2013/en/papa-francesco
-cotidie_20131007_fleeing-god_en.html by *L'Osservatore Romano*, weekly ed. in
English, n. 41, 9 October 2013

80. http://www.vatican.va/holy_father/francesco/cotidie/2013/en/papa-francesco
-cotidie_20131007_fleeing-god_en.html by *L'Osservatore Romano*, weekly ed. in
English, n. 41, 9 October 2013

81. http://www.vatican.va/holy_father/francesco/homilies/2013/documents/papa
-francesco_20131013_omelia-giornata-mariana_en.html

82. http://www.vatican.va/holy_father/francesco/homilies/2013/documents/papa
-francesco_20131013_omelia-giornata-mariana_en.html

83. http://www.vatican.va/holy_father/francesco/homilies/2013/documents/papa
-francesco_20131013_omelia-giornata-mariana_en.html

84. http://www.vatican.va/holy_father/francesco/angelus/2013/documents/papa-francesco
_angelus_20131020_en.html

85. https://twitter.com/Pontifex

86. http://www.vatican.va/holy_father/francesco/angelus/2013/documents/papa-francesco
_angelus_20131101_en.html

87. http://www.vatican.va/holy_father/francesco/angelus/2013/documents/papa-francesco
_angelus_20131110_en.html

88. http://www.vatican.va/holy_father/francesco/angelus/2013/documents/papa-francesco
_angelus_20131117_en.html

89. http://www.vatican.va/holy_father/francesco/messages/pont-messages/2013/documents/
papa-francesco_20131121_videomessaggio-festival-dottrina-sociale_en.html#

90. http://www.vatican.va/holy_father/francesco/apost_exhortations/documents/papa
-francesco_esortazione-ap_20131124_evangelii-gaudium_en.html

91. http://www.vatican.va/holy_father/francesco/apost_exhortations/documents/papa
-francesco_esortazione-ap_20131124_evangelii-gaudium_en.html#I.%E2%80%82A
_joy_ever_new,_a_joy_which_is_shared

92. http://www.vatican.va/holy_father/francesco/apost_exhortations/documents/papa
-francesco_esortazione-ap_20131124_evangelii-gaudium_en.html

93. http://www.vatican.va/holy_father/francesco/apost_exhortations/documents/papa
-francesco_esortazione-ap_20131124_evangelii-gaudium_en.html

94. http://www.vatican.va/holy_father/francesco/apost_exhortations/documents/papa
-francesco_esortazione-ap_20131124_evangelii-gaudium_en.html

95. http://www.vatican.va/holy_father/francesco/apost_exhortations/documents/papa
-francesco_esortazione-ap_20131124_evangelii-gaudium_en.html

96. http://www.vatican.va/holy_father/francesco/apost_exhortations/documents/papa
-francesco_esortazione-ap_20131124_evangelii-gaudium_en.html

97. http://www.vatican.va/holy_father/francesco/apost_exhortations/documents/papa
-francesco_esortazione-ap_20131124_evangelii-gaudium_en.html

98. https://twitter.com/Pontifex

99. http://www.vatican.va/holy_father/francesco/angelus/2013/documents/papa-francesco
_angelus_20131201_en.html

100. https://twitter.com/Pontifex

101. http://www.vatican.va/holy_father/francesco/messages/sick/documents/papa
-francesco_20131206_giornata-malato_en.html

102. http://www.vatican.va/holy_father/francesco/messages/pont-messages/2013/documents/
papa-francesco_20131209_videomessaggio-campagna-contro-fame_en.html#

103. https://twitter.com/Pontifex

104. http://www.vatican.va/holy_father/francesco/messages/peace/documents/papa
-francesco_20131208_messaggio-xlvii-giornata-mondiale-pace-2014_en.html

105. http://www.vatican.va/holy_father/francesco/messages/peace/documents/papa
-francesco_20131208_messaggio-xlvii-giornata-mondiale-pace-2014_en.html

106. http://www.vatican.va/holy_father/francesco/angelus/2014/documents/papa-francesco
_angelus_20140101_en.html#

107. https://twitter.com/Pontifex

108. http://www.vatican.va/holy_father/francesco/angelus/2014/documents/papa-francesco
_angelus_20140112_en.html#

109. https://twitter.com/Pontifex

110. http://www.vatican.va/holy_father/francesco/angelus/2014/documents/papa-francesco
_angelus_20140119_en.html#

111. http://www.vatican.va/holy_father/francesco/homilies/2014/documents/papa
-francesco_20140119_omelia-parrocchia-sacro-cuore-gesu_en.html#

112. http://www.vatican.va/holy_father/francesco/messages/youth/documents/papa
-francesco_20140121_messaggio-giovani_2014_en.html

113. http://www.vatican.va/holy_father/francesco/messages/youth/documents/papa
-francesco_20140121_messaggio-giovani_2014_en.html

114. http://www.vatican.va/holy_father/francesco/messages/youth/documents/papa
-francesco_20140121_messaggio-giovani_2014_en.html

115. http://www.vatican.va/holy_father/francesco/messages/youth/documents/papa
-francesco_20140121_messaggio-giovani_2014_en.html

116. http://www.vatican.va/holy_father/francesco/angelus/2014/documents/papa-francesco
_angelus_20140126_en.html#

117. https://twitter.com/Pontifex

118. http://www.vatican.va/holy_father/francesco/angelus/2014/documents/papa-francesco
_angelus_20140209_en.html#

119. http://www.vatican.va/holy_father/francesco/cotidie/2014/en/papa-francesco
-cotidie_20140214_beyond-difficulties_en.html#

120. http://www.vatican.va/holy_father/francesco/angelus/2014/documents/papa-francesco
_angelus_20140216_en.html

121. http://www.vatican.va/holy_father/francesco/homilies/2014/documents/papa
-francesco_20140216_omelia-parrocchia-san-tommaso-apostolo_en.html#

122. http://www.vatican.va/holy_father/francesco/angelus/2014/documents/papa-francesco
_angelus_20140302_en.html#

123. http://www.vatican.va/holy_father/francesco/angelus/2014/documents/papa-francesco
_angelus_20140302_en.html#

124. http://www.vatican.va/holy_father/francesco/homilies/2014/documents/papa
-francesco_20140305_omelia-ceneri_en.html

125. http://www.vatican.va/holy_father/francesco/homilies/2014/documents/papa
-francesco_20140305_omelia-ceneri_en.html

If you enjoyed this book, visit

www.tarcherbooks.com

and sign up for Tarcher's e-newsletter to receive
special offers, giveaway promotions, and
information on hot upcoming releases.

TARCHER
PENGUIN

Great Lives Begin with Great Ideas

Connect with the Tarcher Community

• • •

Stay in touch with favorite authors!

Enter weekly contests!

Read exclusive excerpts!

Voice your opinions!

Follow us

Tarcher Books

@TarcherBooks